● CONNECTING YOU TO W●NDERLANDS

japan

A guidebook to Special Places

photography by
Takashi Sato

This Edition first published in 2019 by MAMUKAI BOOKS GALLERY,
a division of Arttrav Inc., Japan.

Photography and text copyright ©2019 by Takashi Sato
Translation copyright ©2019 by Stella Colucci
All rights reserved.

Cataloging in publication data: National Diet Library, Japan

ISBN 978 4 904 40218 4 (pbk)
ISBN 978 4 904 40222 1 (pbk)
ISBN 978 4 904 40219 1 (ebk)
ISBN 978 4 904 40220 7 (pod)

Book Design by Sankakusha Inc.

International Marketing by Arttrav North America
801 Second Avenue, Suite 800
Seattle, Washington, USA

https://www.wonderlandsgo.com

Printed in Japan

1 2 3 4 5 6 7 8 9 10

DISCLAIMER

The *Connecting You to Wonderlands* series is designed to take you to places of wonderment. We offer general information as well as insights for the international traveler. While the author and publisher have made every effort to provide current information as of printing, things are always changing. If we missed something, please be forgiving and let us know about it.

How to use this book

1 Location page headings
The heading of each location page shows the name of the town, the prefecture, the area in Japan where the place is located, and also the best time to visit.

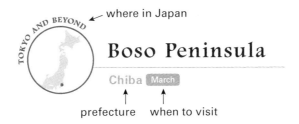

where in Japan
prefecture
when to visit

2 More information at your fingertips
On pages 8 through 93, directions are provided on how to get to the locations by the most convenient way. The URL listed here is for that location's official website if one is available in English and/or other languages. Each locale publishes its own website so content will differ from site to site.

In addition, the QR code in the bottom right corner of each chapter title page links directly to the book's website page at https://www.wonderlandsgo.com. Use a QR code reading app on your smartphone and scan the code. More information on the corresponding location will appear, putting maps, directions, seasonal highlights, things to do nearby and other interesting tidbits at your fingertips.

3 Area features
On some pages, the author takes you further into the deep corners of Japan. VENTURING OUT, TRAVEL NOTES and WHY IT'S SPECIAL explain a little more about that particular area. Get to know some of the interesting features in that locale under these headings.

4 Good To Know
Traveling around the countryside is a little different from city centers. In **Chapter 5 Good To Know**, we compiled a few notes on what to expect and what is expected. On pages 78-93 are a few suggested itineraries. Use the QR code on page 77 and jump to the book's website for additional information.

5 Searching for information online
Do make use of good references available online. The more popular destinations will successfully display search results, but sometimes a less popular location, or a place name that has a homonymous noun, will need help. Try adding JAPAN after the name of the place. For example, instead of "Kagura" by itself, enter "Kagura Japan" for a successful search.

Contents

1 Northeast of Tokyo

1. Boso Peninsula, Chiba — 08
2. Okutama, Tokyo — 10
3. Hydrangea Haven, Kanagawa — 12
4. Numazu, Shizuoka — 14
5. Minuma Tanbo, Saitama — 15
6. Mt. Akagi, Gunma — 16
7. Lake Hibara, Fukushima — 18
8. Izunuma, Miyagi — 19
9. Tono, Iwate — 20

2 Hokkaido to Honshu

10. Kushiro, Hokkaido — 22
11. Lake Toya, Hokkaido — 25
12. Hagurosan, Yamagata — 26
13. Akiyamago, Niigata — 28
14. Nagaoka, Niigata — 30
15. Azumino, Nagano — 32
16. Hakuba, Northern Alps, Nagano — 34
17. Southern Alps, Yamanashi — 35
18. Noto Peninsula, Ishikawa — 37
19. Gokayama, Toyama — 38
20. Kazura Bridge, Fukui — 39
21. Korankei, Aichi — 40

3 Honshu to Western Japan

22. Fuden Pass, Mie — 42
23. Kumano Kodo, Wakayama — 44
24. Mt. Yoshino, Nara — 46
25. Lake Biwa, Shiga — 47
26. Miyama, Kyoto — 48
27. Nose, Osaka — 49
28. Mushiake Bay, Okayama — 51
29. Mt. Daisen, Tottori — 52
30. Ini Rice Terraces, Hiroshima — 54

4 Shikoku & Kyushu

31. Sanuki Fuji, Kagawa — 58
32. Shimanto River, Kochi — 59
33. Ochiai Village, Tokushima — 60
34. Hakata Island, Ehime — 62
35. Yame Tea Fields, Fukuoka — 64
36. Hiraodai, Fukuoka — 65
37. Chikugo River Drawbridge, Saga — 66
38. Kujuku Islands, Nagasaki — 68
39. Aso, Kumamoto — 70
40. Nagasakibana, Oita — 72
41. Takachiho, Miyazaki — 74
42. Sakurajima, Kagoshima — 75

MAP IS NOT TO SCALE

5 Good To Know

In the Countryside	78
References Online	80
Modes of Transportation	82
Favorite Itineraries	88
Things To Do	92

WHY IT'S SPECIAL

Festivals in Japan	17
Hokkaido's Local Foods	24
Travel Routes	36
Rice Terraces	50
About satoyama	56
Preserving the Harvest	69
Zekkei	76

The author, your personal guide

©Satoki Fujimura

Takashi Sato has been capturing stunning images of Japan for three decades. He has traveled to some of the most remote locations in all 47 prefectures to catch the many faces of Japan on film. In recent years, Mr. Sato has focused on subjects and vistas that are classically Japanese. His work is in demand among collectors and publishers.

1
Northeast of Tokyo

Boso Peninsula

Chiba March

The Boso Peninsula has a warm and temperate climate. Spring comes early here. Canola flowers (*nanohana*) start blooming in February. By March, they are everywhere. Especially in the Ishigami district, the canola fields seem to go on forever. These flowers have a distinctly brilliant yellow shade that easily marks the first sign of spring. Local residents take special

TRAVEL NOTES

The Japanese *nanohana* is actually the rapeseed plant, part of the same family as baby broccoli. The best time to see the yellow blooms in this area would be March to April. *Torokko* trains run on the weekends. Pamphlets in English are available from the local tourist information office at the Yoro Keikoku train station.

care in growing them along the tracks of the Kominato and Isumi Railways. When you see that quaint little train on the Kominato Line running through the sea of bright yellow blooms, just imagine it spreading Happiness as it goes by.

GETTING THERE A 10-minute walk from Yoro Keikoku Station on Kominato Railways.

Okutama

TOKYO AND BEYOND

Tokyo May November

Tokyo, the capital of Japan. From its center eastward, modern buildings stand alongside commercial facilities and residential areas. By contrast, natural beauty has been preserved within the surrounding hills to the West. Tama has one of the most beautiful examples of *satoyama*, the traditional rural landscape resulting from the codependency of the land and its inhabitants. Mount Takao has splendid views of the mountains. Okutama is full of forests, gorges and waterfalls.

A visit to these outskirts of Tokyo will surprise you with the wonders of nature. The woods are endless. Perhaps you might want to soak up the fresh air by hiking through the trails, or go cycling, or enjoy a barbecue in the picnic areas. In May, forest trees start to fill out with sprouting buds. Pale young leaves turn to all different shades of green in the summer. In the fall, the hardwoods show off brilliant golds and reds as the leaves start to turn, and the colorful foliage draws many visitors in mid-November. Roads can get quite congested on weekends and holidays when the autumn leaves peak.

GETTING THERE A half-hour walk from Hatonosu train station.
● Okutama Visitor Center https://www.gotokyo.org/en/spot/314/

TRAVEL NOTES

The Okutama area can be reached by train on the JR Ome Line from any of the 13 stops between Ome and Okutama stations. A scenic walk between Hatonosu and Shiromaru stations will take about an hour on the footpath by Tama River. Some areas of the footpath can be tricky with rock formations so be sure to wear comfortable shoes. Stop at Shiromaru Dam and Hatonosu Gorge along the way.

TOKYO AND BEYOND

Hydrangea Haven

Kanagawa June

June is rainy season in Japan. Wet and humid days continue, raining all the time. Water loving flowers are full of life during this damp time of year, especially hydrangeas, which look their best in the rain. The town of Kaisei in western Kanagawa is famous for hydrangeas growing by the ridge of rice paddies. Starting in late June, about 5,000 bushes break out in soft pastel snowballs of blue, purple, pink and white for two weeks or so.

A walk in the rain can actually be quite nice; opening the umbrella when it starts to rain, putting it away when it stops. If you peek into a hydrangea bush, a snail on a leaf might be hard at work, doing whatever snails do. In the rice paddies, birds might be digging for worms. And when the skies clear, turning blue-gray to pink in the west, Mt. Fuji's outline might appear if you squint hard enough.

GETTING THERE 7 minutes by bus from Shin Matsuda train station on the Odakyu Line; or a 20-minute walk from Kaisei train station.

VENTURING OUT

| **Miura Beach** | The sandy beaches of Miura are crowded with oceangoing swimmers in the summer. In the winter (November to February), white *daikon* radishes line up to dry on a corner of the beach like a local seasonal reminder. Sea breezes and plenty of sunshine enrich the flavor of the radishes before they are preserved in *nuka*, a fermented rice bran. The result: delicious *takuan* pickles. The ocean is somewhat warmer in the Kanto region. Still, the winter mornings can be harsh and it helps to dress warm. And the sun can feel so good!

TOKYO AND BEYOND

Numazu

Shizuoka

The Izu Peninsula is easily accessible from the Tokyo metro area. It has a pleasant climate year round. The ocean, the beaches, the mountains, hot springs, great food, and an assortment of places to stay make it a popular getaway destination. At the western end of the peninsula, in Nishi Izu, a diverse geographical terrain is composed of the clear blue Pacific, rocky cliffs and little beaches. The coastal road boasts a scenic drive, but beware of some of the narrow passages. From Kirameki Hill (this view), Suruga Bay and Mt. Fuji can be seen in the distance. Directly below, the miniscule village and port of Ita look cozy. Other overlooks—Cape Deai, Yubae Hill, Kenko-no-Mori and Midori Hill— also boast a scenic view of Mt. Fuji across the bay.

GETTING THERE For Kirameki Hill, less than an hour by bus from Shuzenji train station on the Izu Hakone Railway. Get off at Heda bus stop, then 10 minutes by taxi.

TOKYO AND BEYOND

Minuma Tanbo
Saitama

Rice paddies, farms and parks make up a huge green space called Minuma Tanbo. For hundreds of years, Tokyo's surface runoff has collected here. The preservation area serves an important environmental function. Residential development is restricted, and the terrain remains very open. Nearby residents treasure the space. They walk along the river, they farm, they play in the park.

    Not far from Higashi Urawa Station on the JR Line, Minuma Tanbo's quintessential gingko leaves at Sakurabashi will start turning gold after summer. The gingko trees lined up in a row create a splendid view. On the bridge, people exchange greetings as they pass each other by. Fishermen carry on conversations as they dangle their lines in the river. Walkers amble through the bamboo groves, bogs and shrines nearby. Heavy moisture finding its way from the river and the wetlands can hang in the air on a misty morning, still promising a sunny day. There is definitely something that cannot be found in the city, that certain *je ne sais quoi* for peaceful reserves.

GETTING THERE From Omiya or Saitama Shin Toshin station, 20 minutes by taxi. Omiya station has a tourist information center.
- More at http://www.minumatanbo-saitama.jp/english/outline.htm
- Saitama Tourism and International Relations Bureau https://www.stib.jp/e/tourism/offices.html

Mt. Akagi

Gunma

Ono, Kono and Kakumanbuchi—these are the three lakes that are central to the generous natural landscapes of Mt. Akagi. Kakumanbuchi is a marsh area in the highlands. Starting at the Akagi Koen Visitors Center entrance and walking all the way around the marsh is a good way to see a number of things, like skunk cabbages in spring and the changing foliage in fall. Summer is the season for rhododendrons. Shades of red appear everywhere, especially at the Akagi Shirakaba Bokujo (it means White Birch Farm) where they grow in large groupings. The flowering bushes keep multiplying because rhododendrons are toxic to livestock and the cows leave them alone. The uphill drive to Mt. Akagi's summit is steep enough by car, but tackling the climb on a bicycle is popular too.

GETTING THERE Kan'etsu Kotsu runs buses from Maebashi train station to Akagiyama Visitors Center bus stop, about an hour's ride. Non-stop buses run on weekends and holidays. On weekdays, you will need to change buses at Fujimi Onsen. The Visitor Center rents bicycles. • **Gunma Bureau of Tourism** https://www.visitgunma.jp/en/
• **JNTO** https://www.japan.travel/en/spot/2077/

WHY IT'S SPECIAL

▸▸ Festivals in Japan

Japan has more than 100,000 local festivals, some with hundreds of years of history. If you come upon a festival during your travels, joining the fun with your local hosts can be a great way to experience traditional culture first hand.

The **Kanuma Aki Matsuri** (Autumn Festival) is held on the second weekend of October at Imamiya Shrine in Kanuma (Tochigi). During this two-day festival, men standing on the roofs of floats adorned with beautiful wooden carvings are paraded around town. This event, called *Yatai Gyoji* (Float Event), is on the UNESCO Intangible Cultural Heritage list.

In Chichibu (Saitama), a festival that has lasted over 400 years is held at Muku Shrine on the second Sunday of October. During **Ryusei Matsuri**, (something akin to the festival of the spirit of the dragon), artisans shoot home made rockets shaped like dragons climbing toward the heavens, seeking the community's good fortune.

For three days at the end of the second week in May, **Otabi Matsuri** (Travel Festival) is celebrated in Komatsu (Ishikawa). The highlight of this festival from the 17th Century is the *kabuki* performed by children on festival floats.

Ryusei Matsuri

Otabi Matsuri

Kanuma Aki Matsuri

NORTHERN HONSHU, PACIFIC COAST

Lake Hibara

Fukushima August

Urabandai is dotted with many lakes and ponds, large and small. Mount Bandai forms a distinct backdrop for one of the most picturesque landscapes in Japan. It is a magnet for photographers seeking to capture natural elements from every imaginable angle. One of the biggest draws might be the frequent morning fog. A popular destination for photo retreats and tours, visitors with all levels of photography skills can take advantage of the services provided by some of the pension hotels that guide their guests to photogenic spots.

Batches of *misohagi* (purple loosetrife) can be found at the campsite on the western shore of Lake Hibara in August. These magenta blooms grow in beachy wetlands during the summer. The hazy shore, the dark edgeline of Mount Bandai and the wildflowers create a beautiful scene in the morning mist. Dragonflies fly around everywhere, leaving lasting impressions for the visitor.

GETTING THERE Take the Ban'etsu West Line to Inawashiro train station, then 30 minutes by bus to Lake Hibara.
• **Sightseeing brochure** https://www.urabandai-inf.com/?page_id=25715

Izunuma

NORTHERN HONSHU, PACIFIC COAST

Miyagi — November - February

Not to be mistaken for the Izu Peninsula in Shizuoka, "Izu"-numa in Miyagi Prefecture is a winter habitat for geese. The greater white-fronted goose, called *magan*, is one of the Natural Monuments of Japan. The large bird has a wingspan that can reach one and a half meters. The best place to watch them fly off in the morning is from the pier at the western edge of the swamp. Daybreak is when the geese are the loudest, flapping their wings wide. Pre-dawn, the birds honk in the distance before take-off time. Small flocks will appear in the sky as it starts to turn light. Some of them will circle over the swamp, while others will head straight for the rice paddies to feed. The Ministry of Environment lists the sound of these geese taking off in large flocks among the 100 Soundscapes of Japan. If a flock happens to pass directly overhead, the experience might even be called a *sense-scape*.

GETTING THERE Izunuma is a 10-minute car ride from Kurikoma Kogen train station (Tohoku Shinkansen). If you take a taxi, be sure to arrange your return ride back to the train station.
- Miyagi travel guide https://www.pref.miyagi.jp/site/kankou-en/
- Izunuma live camera feed http://www.sizenken.biodic.go.jp/view.php?camera_no=90

Tono

Iwate June

Tono is known for its folk tales, its pastoral landscapes, its gentle people. It is an interesting stop in the Tohoku region. There is also something else. Tono runs steam locomotives every so often, although the event calendar is not always well publicized. Consider it luck to drive by and stumble upon the actual date when a steam engine runs against horses!

The local horse club sponsors this special event once a year on a Saturday in mid-June. Many photographers visit Tono for that purpose and vie for a good spot to plant their tripods. They wait patiently, peeking through the viewfinder over and over to make sure their camera is perfectly positioned. As the train approaches the crowd, the sounds of the steam engine grow louder. The train gets closer. It comes into sight...first the puffs of steam, then the train itself, and then three horses racing the train alongside the tracks. Cameras click all about, and then the train and horses flash by. What a rush for the bystanders!

GETTING THERE From Shin Hanamaki (JR Tohoku Shinkansen), transfer to the Kamaishi Line for Tono station.
• Tono Tourism Assocation http://www.tonojikan.jp/Several_languages/english/english.html

2
Hokkaido to Honshu

TO SEE MORE FROM CHAPTER 2, SCAN THIS QR CODE

Kushiro

Hokkaido December - February

Kushiro Shitsugen is famous for Japanese Cranes. It is a breeding ground. Admirers of these red-headed birds (*tancho*) specifically go to the Otowa Bridge on Kushiro River, where nests can be observed from a distance.

Just before dawn, in the faint light, the bodies of dozens of cranes start to take shape. It is freezing cold in December, more than 20 degrees below Centigrade, cold enough to numb the hands. It is worth it, though. Nature in winter is absolutely beautiful. The mist rises from the river to form icicles on the trees. The morning rays hit the river's surface like a drop of red dye. Diamond dust floats in the air. When sunlight touches the cranes, they will start to bustle with activity, filling the air with their cries. Gradually, a few at a time, they will fly off to feed. Watching them is awesome, and their size is astonishing when they spread their wings.

You can view the cranes at close range from the Tsurumi-dai observation area and also at the sanctuary. Both feeding grounds are in the village of Tsurui-mura. No doubt these adorable creatures will warm your heart.

TRAVEL NOTES

If you have two to three days, start from Kushiro Wetlands to take in some interesting sights in and around Lake Akan and Lake Mashu. Up-to-date local travel information is available in English from one of the four tourist centers in Kushiro city. Hokkaido attracts visitors year round, from summer drives to winter sports. Access to Kushiro is more convenient now with budget flights between Osaka and Kushiro priced at around 10,000 yen.

GETTING THERE For Tsurui-mura, the bus ride from Kushiro train station is about an hour to Tsurumi-dai bus stop. The sanctuary is a 15-minute walk from Tsurui-mura Yakuba bus stop. ● **Kushiro-Lake Akan** http://en.kushiro-lakeakan.com/overview/ ● **Hokkaido Tourism** http://en.visit-hokkaido.jp

Konbu farming in Akkeshi

Potato fields in Biei

WHY IT'S SPECIAL
▸▸ Hokkaido's Local Foods

Hokkaido is a wonderland of food. Bounties of the earth include potatoes, corn, melons, haskap berries. Dairy products such as milk, cheese and butter are especially rich in taste. Fruits of the sea include crabs, salmon, scallops, oysters, sea urchins, abalone, seaweed. These are but a few of the foods that are local goodies from northern Japan.

There are many types of *konbu* (edible seaweed), and Hokkaido has its share of homegrown varieties. They come in different shapes, sizes and tastes. In Akkeshi, *konbu* farming takes place between June and October. After the seaweed is harvested from the seas, the small fishing boats return to the harbor. Unloading the harvest is no easy feat. The kelp needs to be pulled taut, then placed on the sand to dry. Sun dried *konbu* results from a process that keeps things busy on the beach. Friends and family, everyone pitches in. When the harvest is good, fully loaded trucks come and go from the port.

Biei is known as Hill Town for its many hills. Wheat, potatoes, corn, onions and beets are some of the crops that are grown in the hilly terrain. This farmfield is ready for potatoes to be planted in May. The tractor has left contoured stripes after plowing the soil. It takes skill and hard work to cultivate the sloping fields for good buttery potatoes.

- Biei Tourism Association https://www.biei-hokkaido.jp/en/

Lake Toya

Hokkaido May

Hokkaido awakens to spring almost overnight. On Honshu, *ume* (plum blossoms) pop open first, followed by *sakura* (cherry blossoms). On this northernmost island of Japan, *ume* and *sakura* open their buds almost at the same time to peak in May. Plum blossoms are the highlight of Sobetsu Park on the southeastern waterfront of Lake Toya. After a long winter, pretty blooms announce the arrival of spring and visitors crowd the park. Sobetsu Park also has cherry trees, so the viewing pleasure can double if the timing is right. Running into a friend or neighbor can be a nice surprise and even more gratifying to have stepped outside.

If the weather cooperates, snow-capped Mt. Yotei will show itself. It is one of many *furusato Fuji*, the local Mt. Fuji look-alike that locals like to claim throughout mountainous Japan.

GETTING THERE Sobetsu Park is a 15-minute bus ride from Toya-ko Onsen bus terminal.
• Toya-ko Onsen Tourist Association http://en.laketoya.com/

Hagurosan

Yamagata

The Three Mountains of Dewa, known as *Dewa Sanzan*, are located in central Yamagata. Gassan, Hagurosan and Yudonosan are sacred mountains that have been at the heart of mountain worship for ages.

A number of inns at the foot of Hagurosan accommodate pilgrims on their long journeys. From Zuishinmon, the pilgrim's path leads the traveler ahead. Snow is deep and all is quiet here in the winter. The pilgrim's path becomes a trail packed down by foot traffic. You can lose your footing in the banks of virgin snow, and staying on the trail can be difficult. Descending the stone steps one by one takes concentration. The sacred environment is purifying: the tall cedars, the gently bubbling brook, the serenity of nature to which we are privileged to bear eye witness.

After crossing the sacred vermillion bridge, a five-storied pagoda will appear in the woods. The wooden structure is a National Treasure. What a wonderment that the tower was built in such an isolated place in the first place, and to still be standing today. Remarkable.

GETTING THERE Shonai Kotsu Bus Line runs from Tsuruoka City. To visit the pagoda, get off at Zuishinmon bus stop (50-minute ride) and head toward the stone steps leading to the pagoda.
• **Hagurosan** https://www.japan-guide.com/e/e7902.html

VENTURING OUT

| **Owarabi Rice Terraces** | Rice is harvested in late September. The stalks are cut, bundled and left to air dry on the stakes. This time-consuming process adds flavor to the grains of rice. Sparrows and crows come looking for a free feast, pecking at the loose grains on the ground. Birds need to feed too, though they can be a nuisance to the rice farmer. Drying methods vary by region. Piling the stalks on a stake is germane to the Tohoku region. If you visit other areas in Japan during this season, take note of the different methods.

GETTING THERE 15 minutes by car from Uzen Yamabe train station.

Akiyamago

Niigata

Upstream of Nakatsugawa River, there is a cluster of small villages known as Akiyamago. Nestled deep in the mountains, the remote community is composed of eight hamlets in Niigata and five hamlets in Nagano. Maekura is one of these hamlets located on the Niigata side in Tsunan. It is especially small with just ten households, the homes forming a circle in an infinite

VENTURING OUT

| **Uonuma** | Known for its production of the *koshihikari* rice variety, Uonuma sees some of the heaviest snowfall in Japan. It snows almost every day in the winter, accumulating up to two meters. You cannot just shovel the snow around here. You have to dig yourself out. Just imagine how much snow there is if you have to climb out of it. Yet people dismiss the battle against the elements as a daily ritual. Life is not easy in these parts; if you grew up in snow country, you would know that well.

Urasa and Koide train stations on the Tadami Line serve the town of Uonuma. Signage can sometimes get lost in the snow, like the railroad crossing near Hirose train station. It stands alone like a toy of many colors. A rabbit could easily hop across the all-white fields looking for playmates. Animals like to play in the snow too, don't they?

bond of the families that live here.

Snow starts to fall daily in late November, piling up to five meters in some places. A path has to be cut into the snow to access the house, just wide enough for one person and taller than most adults. The hamlet is very quiet under the thick white blanket, as if all sounds had somehow left. But when you hear the sound of trickling water, it means spring is around the corner. As the snow starts to melt, plants sprout and the local mountain vegetables come into season. If you are visiting there in springtime, you have to try the mountain vegetables. By mid-October, autumn starts to show its colors; then winter returns.

GETTING THERE About 40 minutes by car from Tsunan rail station.

Nagaoka
Niigata August

The fireworks display at Nagaoka is part of a festival that memorializes those who perished in conflicts and natural disasters. The Nagaoka Festival is an occasion to mourn, to wish for speedy restoration, and to hope for peace. Held on August 2 and 3 every year, the Nagaoka Festival Great Fireworks Display illuminates the banks of Japan's longest Shinano River with a magnificent show of fireworks. It has to be one of the best in Japan. Different shapes and colors burst open one after another, exploding like artwork in the sky. As the show comes to a close, during the climax where layer upon layer of dazzling shapes explode in the summer's night sky, the sighs, cheers and applause fuse into a single roar—the voice of approval from the audience.

CENTRAL HONSHU

Azumino

Nagano

Cold water springs flowing from underground aquifers get filled by snowmelt in the Northern Alps. In Azumino, that natural spring water is perfect for cultivating *wasabi*. Tadegawa, the river that flows through the city, is the key to some nostalgic charm. The focal point is a set of three water wheels that were originally constructed for famed director Akira Kurosawa's movie, *Yume* (Dream). As the slow turning wheels reflect in the gently rippling river, they evoke an image from Japan's yesteryear.

The water wheels can be visited at the riverside Daio Wasabi Farm. Visitors are welcome to roam the huge complex. The parking lot is spacious, and the farm is popular with tourists. The small white flowers on the *wasabi* plants bloom from late March to early April. Fresh *wasabi* aside, other products made with the pungent green horseradish, like *wasabi* ice cream, are offered at the store on the farm.

Azumino is near many popular destinations. In addition to mountain getaways in Hakuba, Kamikochi and the Japan Alps, historical landmarks such as Matsumoto Castle and Zenkoji Temple are interesting to tour.

GETTING THERE To Daio Wasabi Farm, 10 minutes by car from Hodaka train station.

TRAVEL NOTES

How about a different perspective from afloat or up in the air? Azumino Kisen operates guided river rides between April and October, weather permitting. You can enjoy land views of the three seasons, and even see the water wheels up close from its waterside. The trip takes about 20 minutes. The company also operates hot air balloon rides during the same period in the Omachi-Matsukawa area, about 30 minutes away. The balloons are tethered so it just goes up and down for a 5-minute ride, but the views from high up in the air are spectacular. For ages 2 and up. No reservations necessary for individuals and small parties.

• More at www.azuminokisen.com

Hakuba, Northern Alps

Nagano

At the foot of northern Japan Alps is a typically Japanese landscape. A scattering of traditional homes decorates a wide valley. This is the village of Hakuba. There are great hiking trails, ski slopes for all levels and a range of facilities for winter sports. Best of all, there are fabulous hot spring resorts.

For a full view of the Hakuba mountain range, Oide Park is the best place to go. Suspended over Himekawa is Oide Bridge. It is an old-fashioned bridge that matches the old-fashioned thatched-roof houses. Go early in the morning while it is still dark. The cold air by the river seems to wrap everything around it. As the sky lightens, the three mountains of Hakuba known as *Hakuba Sanzan* start to take shape: Shiroumayaridake, Shakushidake and Shiroumadake. Their snow-capped peaks are a refreshing sight.

GETTING THERE Express buses from Nagano train station to Hakuba village take 70 minutes. Get off at Hakuba Ekimae bus stop (Hakuba train station). ● **Tourism Commission of Hakuba Village** http://www.hakubavalley.jp/index_english.html

Southern Alps

Yamanashi

Hokuto city is a prime example of the beautiful landscapes found in Yatsugatake and the Southern Alps. The vista goes on and on during a scenic drive along one of the main roads known as the Shichiriiwa Line. On this scenic route, Suishanosato Park is an easy stop for viewing the bold lines of Kaikomadake. There are several peaks throughout Japan that are named Komadake, but Kaikomadake is the tallest at 2,970 meters above sea level. Rice paddies can be seen on the gentle slopes, and the sky looks bigger. When the azalea hedges in the park turn bright red in the fall, it will not be long before the mount turns white with snow. Do visit the 2,000-year-old giant cherry tree in neighboring Jissoji Temple if you are in the area when it blooms. Yamanashi is famous for growing some of the most delectable fruits, yielding the highest production in Japan for summer peaches and fall grapes.

GETTING THERE 10 minutes by taxi from Hinoharu train station.
- Hokuto Tourism Organization https://www.hokuto-kanko.jp/visit_hokuto.html

WHY IT'S SPECIAL

▸▸ Travel Routes

Most tourists see Japan by taking what is coined in the travel industry as the Golden Route. The typical itinerary might start with a tour of Tokyo and its environs after arriving at Haneda or Narita International Airport, then jumping on the bullet train and stopping at Hakone, Mt. Fuji, Nagoya and Kyoto along the Tokaido Line. The tour usually ends in Osaka with a flight home from Kansai International Airport. But the tourist's options are not limited to this predictable pattern. There are more itineraries that cover different regions, bundling some of the other "best of Japan."

The Dragon Route, for example, cuts right through the middle. The way this particular itinerary climbs northerly in the shape of a dragon gives meaning to its name. It winds through the natural beauty found in the Japan Alps, to famous geothermal spa towns like Gero Hot Springs and to many historically preserved townships. A different side of Japan can be experienced in the temperate areas surrounding the Seto Inland Sea by way of the Setouchi Route. Or yet, the small hamlets in the hollows deep in the mountainous region could be the next destination tour into the Deep North. The way to explore Japan can also be through special interests and themes. More travel routes, as suggested by the author and publishing staff, begin on P88.

No matter where, no matter how, Japan is a wonderland of hidden gems awaiting your visit. For details on the routes mentioned here, visit the following websites.

- **The Dragon Route** https://www.dragonroute.net/dragon_e/
- **Setouchi: The Inland Sea** http://setouchifinder.com/inland-sea/en/
- **Deep North of Japan** http://deepnorthjapan.org/

Noto Peninsula

Ishikawa

In the villages of Osawa and Kami-Osawa, the homes have an interesting feature. A hedge of dried bamboo is placed around the house as insulation from the severe winter winds that blow from the Japan Sea. It also helps to cool the house in the summer. This type of *kakine*, or hedge, is made of a tall and slender bamboo known as *nigadake*. The bamboo hedge is called *magaki*, and if the entire length of the bamboo is used, the tied panels can reach four meters high.

Swallows will sometimes squeeze in and out of the *magaki* through slivers of space between the bamboo. In Japan, swallows making their nests in and around the house are a sign of good fortune. Village scenes like this are preserved as valuable cultural landscapes.

GETTING THERE 30 minutes by bus or car from Michi no Eki rest stop in Wajima.

CENTRAL HONSHU

Gokayama

Toyama

Although lesser known than Shirakawago in Gifu Prefecture, Gokayama in neighboring Toyama is a group of 40 small villages, two of which have been designated as UNESCO World Heritage Sites. Nestled in the hills at the end of the path, the cluster is much smaller in scale than Shirakawago. It definitely feels like uncharted territory. The *gassho-zukuri* architecture features a steep pitch that emphasizes the overwhelming size of the thatched roof. Fire safety is a serious business, so smoking is permitted in designated areas only. Preservation is a collective effort.

Residents live a simple life in these enclaves, maintaining the traditional way of life in remote rural Japan. They are exceptionally kind to the curious visitor. If you stay at a home that has been converted to a B&B, you might be able to explore the attic that was designed with plenty of space for cultivating silkworms. A warm open fireplace in the floor could be the perfect setting for overnight guests to gather around for meals and stories. A chorus of frogs might even provide evening entertainment when the rice paddies are flooded in May. A trail leads to an overlook, about a 10-minute walk. At certain times of the year, night lights make the entire village sparkle. If you make the climb in the dark, be sure to take a flashlight.

GETTING THERE The World Heritage Bus is a dedicated bus service running from Johana train station to the two UNESCO villages of Ainokura and Suganuma. The ride takes about 30 minutes. *This view: Ainokura Village*
• **Gokayama Travel Guide** http://gokayama-info.jp/en/

CENTRAL HONSHU

Kazura Bridge

Fukui

This *kazura-bashi* (woven vine bridge) may not be as famous as the one in Tokushima, but it can certainly compete as one of the more beautiful specimens of simple suspension bridges that are handmade. Craftsmen recreated the original bridge using special materials brought to the site. The vines woven together to make this bridge are a specific type called *shirakuchi kazura*.

The prospect of seeing something old and new in the Fukui area can be inspiring if you are not familiar with this place. Step forward on the planks of the bridge and you can see the river under your feet between the 10-centimeter spacings. Hold on to the vine railings, but be careful; they are thick and hard to grab. It will be quite a thrill for the adventurous to cross a swaying bridge. Maybe not for everyone; you might prefer standing back as a spectator. Albeit a man-made element, the organic bridge assimilates itself into the autumn forest to look very natural in its setting.

GETTING THERE 30 minutes by car from Takefu train station. The bridge is closed from December to March due to heavy snow; also closed in bad weather.
• Ikeda Farm Village Tourist Association https://e-ikeda-e.jp/en/

Korankei

Aichi November

Korankei is famous for its autumn colors. It is full of nature and a great place to relax in any season, but autumn is tops. Thousands of *momiji* (Japanese maples) representing many different varieties fill the entire valley with glorious color. There are many good autumn viewing spots in the valley: Taigetsu Bridge, Koshakuji Temple, Asuke Yashiki Village. When the sun is out, the color contrast is bright. When it rains, the fall colors look more subtle. At night, spotlights give the leaves a shine.

Alongside the river is a path crowned with burnished leaves on overhanging branches. A walk on this path feels like passing under a ceiling adorned with jeweled ornaments. A stunning mirror image of the brilliant *momiji* forest reflects in the water.

A half-hour drive from Korankei in Obara is a well known garden of cherry blossoms that rebloom in autumn. Catching the fall foliage and the cherry blossoms in one visit is like getting two for one, so do try to visit both Korankei and Obara. To avoid the traffic, time your visits early in the day.

GETTING THERE For Korankei: Meitetsu Bus Line runs from Toyota-shi train station on the Meitetsu Mikawa Line; 45 minutes to Korankei bus stop. For Obara: Take the Toyota Oiden Bus for an hour ride from Toyota-shi train station to Obara Okusa bus stop.

3
Honshu to Western Japan

TO SEE MORE FROM CHAPTER 3, SCAN THIS QR CODE

Fuden Pass

Mie Autumn-Spring

Fu-den oroshi is the Japanese term for katabatic winds that blow in the southern part of Mie Prefecture. These downslope winds come in the fall and last through spring. Winds blow when the air is colder on the mountain surface than the surrounding air, usually in the morning in fair

weather.

    First, a large blanket of fog covers the mountain ridge before dawn. The fog drops really fast, at times tipping down to the village while causing serious atmospheric changes. And then the winds come. The fog continues to drift for several hours. If you want to capture this natural phenomenon on camera, try using long exposure and set it for 10 seconds to get a closer perspective. Experiencing the real thing will be a moving experience, much more than what the photograph can show.

GETTING THERE To see the katabatic winds, take the Kumano Kodo Seiryusosen bus line from JR Kumano-shi train station for a 30-minute ride to Takachira bus stop. The Oroshi district is a 10-minute walk.

Kumano Kodo

Wakayama

Kumano Kodo is a network of old pilgrimage roads. Through the mountains or by the sea, the pilgrimage routes spread in several directions. Nakahechi is one of the more popular routes taken by pilgrims and tourists.

Around the Toganoki Chaya, the same views from years past remain brilliantly unchanged. Fall foliage is at its peak in November, when sunlight filters through the multi-colored leaves to start the day. Someone was walking his dog early; a *Kishu*, an ancient local breed. *Ohayo gozaimasu!* The morning greeting is always crisp and clear, automatically launching into conversation.

The visitor can quickly feel welcome and comfortable deep in the mountains of the Kinki region, where historical Japanese style homes and a traditional lifestyle are proud marks of endurance.

GETTING THERE Kii Tanabe, Nachi and Shingu train stations are entry points for Kumano Kodo. For the Nakahechi route, Ryujin and Meiko Bus Lines run from Kii Tanabe train station. The bus ride is 45 minutes to Nakahechi Bijutsukan-mae, in front of the Nakahechi Museum.
- **Kumano Tourism Bureau** http://www.tb-kumano.jp/en/
- **Kumano Travel** https://www.kumano-travel.com/en

VENTURING OUT

| **Aragijima** | Viewed from the observation point across the river, the rice terraces at Aragijima have the peculiar shape of an "island" formed by the meandering river in the town of Aridagawa, Wakayama. Arable land being at a premium in Japan, every inch that can be cultivated will be farmed.

GETTING THERE One hour by bus (Arida Tetsudo Bus Line) to Shimizu bus stop.

Mt. Yoshino

Nara Autumn

Although Mt. Yoshino is one of the most famous places in Japan for cherry blossoms, it can be just as alluring off season. Go to the observation deck at Nakasenbon and watch the fog lift gently off the mountain. If it rained the night before, Kongozan Temple will be revealed in the morning mist like an esoteric portrait. The cherry trees are beautiful, blooms or no blooms. Still wet from the rain, the vivid array of red, orange and yellow leaves have a glossy coating.

Mt. Yoshino is accessible by train and cable car. Comfortable walking shoes are a must for the trek on dirt roads and up the hills. After soaking in the views, hike through the trails and visit landmarks and historical sites. An overdue respite will come with a meal break relished with warm smiles from the shopkeepers of traditional storefronts.

GETTING THERE From Kintetsu Yoshino train station, connect to Senbonguchi cable car station for a 3-minute climb to Mt. Yoshino. Buses also run from the train station; the ride to Cable Yoshinoyama bus stop takes 15 minutes.
• Mt. Yoshino Tourist Association http://www.yoshinoyama-sakura.jp/english/

KANSAI

Lake Biwa

Shiga

Lake Biwa is the largest lake in Japan and the third oldest lake in the world. There are a number of tourist attractions and historical sites around this important water source for the Keihanshin area (Kyoto, Osaka and Kobe). Birdwatching is popular on the northwestern shore. The sun setting behind Chikubu Island is a view worth the wait.

Even if the weather is not the best, shafts of sunlight will manage to break through the clouds. The beams of light shining on Chikubu Island can look absolutely divine.

Venture over to the docks. You might make new friends with the fishermen there. At the least, you will find landscapes and real life images that have remained unchanged for generations.

GETTING THERE Nagahama Port is near the train station. Jump on the Biwako Kisen ferry over to Chikubu Island.
• Shiga Tourism Official Website https://en.biwako-visitors.jp/

Miyama

Kyoto

An hour and a half drive from Kyoto city is a place that looks a little different from the elegant landscape of the ancient capital. At the heart of prefectural Kyoto-fu is an idyllic village in the valley. Miyama is known for the well-preserved homes that proudly display the iconic thatched roof that tops traditional Japanese architecture. These homes were being built with the idea of integrating them into the natural environment long before sustainable homes became today's hot topic. Various trees and bushes in and around the village decorate the scenery through the seasons, like weeping cherries, hydrangeas, *soba* blooms and cosmos flowers. The vintage red mailbox that greets everyone entering the village is not a box at all, but in fact, a cylinder-shaped mail receptacle. It has been there for years, connecting the past with the future.

GETTING THERE From Hiyoshi train station, 40 minutes by city bus to Kita Kayabuki bus stop.
• Miyama Tourism Association https://kyotomiyama.jp/en/

Nose

Osaka

Japan's second largest city, Osaka, is within the prefectural district of Osaka-fu. In contrast to urban Osaka, the northern and southern parts of Osaka-fu are filled with beautiful natural landscapes. Nose is one such place, a rustic pocket in the northernmost sector. Driving away from the city on winding mountain roads, the *sato* landscape, the Japanese countryside, comes into view as rice paddies take over.

The Rice Terraces of Nagatani have been maintained with great care for generations, and rice is produced to this day on ancestral lands. Each terrace is shaped thin and long. A narrow path leads up the hill, the paddies extending in a gentle curve that draws the eye around the bend. Around the neatly ascending rows, large thatched-roof homes can be spotted here and there. There is a stillness to this place, a slower pace of life, that makes it hard to believe that the bustling city is so close.

GETTING THERE Visit the Rice Terraces of Nagatani by Nose Electric Railway to Yamashita train station, then 30 minutes by Hankyu Bus to Morigami bus stop. • **Nose Town Tourism** http://www.town-of-nose.jp/en/

WHY IT'S SPECIAL

▸▸ Rice Terraces

Matsudai/Matsunoyama District (Tokamachi, Niigata): Just 15 terraces are left in this rice growing region. Hoshitoge just got its first snow in this photo. A sea cloud will form in June and September for even more fabulous views.

"Rice paddies on shelves" would be the transliteration of *tanada* (rice terraces). What a great description! Farmers all over the world have been carving out arable space from the side of a hill for thousands of years. To this day, terraced farming can be found across several continents.

In Japan, it is usually reserved for growing rice. Small patches of rice paddies are stepped along the contours of the land, creating lines that meander into the distance. Owarabi (P26), Nose (P48) and Ini (P54) are some of the few hundred *tanada* that are still active. The work is almost all manual because machines are hard to fit. Irrigation is usually unchallenged as water flows downward, and good drainage produces an outstanding crop.

Rice terraces are one of the classic sights of Japan. The best views are from the higher elevations looking down, when the sunlight is more gentle early in the morning or at dusk.

Kunugidaira (Asahi, Yamagata): About 200 paddies fan out on a moderate slope.

Oyama Senmaida (Kamogawa, Chiba): Abstract contours create a random pattern from about 300 plots of various sizes.

Mushiake Bay

Okayama

Oyster rafts floating on Mushiake Bay are the quintessential landscape of the Seto Inland Sea. The famous sight attracts many people to shoot the dawn view. In fact, it has a title just like a painting, called *Mushiake Seto no Akebono* (Seto at Dawn). You will need to drive up the winding road to Mt. Ohira and get there before the sun starts to peek over the horizon. Park at the Ohiradai observation point, which is a really good spot. You might meet a few photography buffs who are already leaving after finishing their shoot. Not to worry; as long as you get there before sunrise, you are not too late. The morning sun will rise over the wide sea and shimmer across the horizon. You can catch the rays of hope just in time. If you go to Mt. Ohira, this particular location is high on the list of recommendations.

GETTING THERE   To Ohiradai observation area: 50 minutes by car from Bicchu Takahashi train station. To view *Mushiake Seto no Akebono* from Mushiake Bay: 40 minutes by bus from Oku train station to Mushiake bus stop.

Mt. Daisen

Tottori

Think of the highlands in western Japan, and the twin resorts of Daisen and Hiruzen come to mind. The two are situated back to back, one in Tottori and the other in Okayama, respectively, and you must go to the other if you visit one. Both resorts are popular among sports enthusiasts: outdoor activities in the summer, snow skiing in the winter. Mt. Daisen has prolific views that can change according to the angle. She can look like Mt. Fuji, or she can have a craggy face. One mountain, multiple looks. Unusual, don't you think?

From the base of Mt. Daisen, in the community known as Mizukue in the town of Kofu, a rural landscape unfolds just below the southern slope. A tiny hut with a thatched roof sits by itself in the middle of the open field. It is a well known landmark and a favorite subject among artists and photographers. When the rainy season ends and the sun is bright, it gets hot enough to break a sweat just standing still. On a lazy summer day, nature can change its temperament in a heartbeat as a fluffy white cloud turns into a huge rain cloud and stretches itself across the sky. The mountain road from this community is a pleasant drive. Views from Kagekake Pass are breathtaking before reaching the sizable forest of beech trees. Here lies a treasure trove of natural effects.

GETTING THERE From Ebi train station, take the town bus to Mizukue bus stop.
• **Tottori Tourism Guide** https://www.tottori-tour.jp/en/

VENTURING OUT

| **Shimane / Yunotsu Hot Springs** | Yunotsu is a two-hour train ride from Ebi station on the Hakubi and Sanin Lines. Yunotsu Onsen (hot springs) itself is part of *Iwami Ginzan Silver Mine and its Cultural Landscape*, a UNESCO World Heritage Site. Yunotsu Port is registered among the 110 Important Preservation Districts for Groups of Traditional Buildings. Yunotsu is an unpretentious hot springs town decorated with Japanese *kanji* signage, giving it a simplistic beauty and a down-home atmosphere.

GETTING THERE 15 minutes on foot from Yunotsu train station.

WESTERN HONSHU

Ini Rice Terraces

Hiroshima

It takes just minutes from the expressway to reach the rice terraces at Ini. In spite of the convenient access, it feels isolated in the mountains. As soon as you come out of a small tunnel, rock walls make a grand stand. The rice terraces in this region are held up by retaining walls built from hand-laid river rocks.

Koinobori (streamers of carp) get hoisted on a pole in the front yard to celebrate Children's Day in May. Each one "swims" in the wind with great purpose. The children must be full of energy in such a household. Maybe the breeze will carry some of that happy energy everywhere. A pick-up truck parked near the house suggests that the adult members of the family are home from working in the fields. Small pick-up trucks seem to add the final touch to the Japanese rural landscape. They are befitting on country roads, playing an important role in agricultural society.

GETTING THERE Highway buses departing from Hiroshima Bus Center stop at the Togouchi exit. Taxis are available for the rest of the way (about 10 minutes).

TRAVEL NOTES

Farm use vehicles in Japan are typically economy size vehicles, as in the small white truck pictured here. Most commercial vehicles seen around town are on a smaller scale too. They take up less room and are ideally suited for Japan's geographical scale; needless to mention, efficient in fuel consumption. The Japanese eco-sense is pervasive, deeply rooted in the concept of *mottainai* (waste not, want not).

> **WHY IT'S SPECIAL**
>
> ▸▸ About *satoyama*

Before the industrial revolution and modernization took over a self-sustained lifestyle, we used to live off the land and let nature be our guide. Somewhere along the way, most of us lost our ties to Mother Earth. In Japan's *satoyama*, though, that connection was never broken. *Sato* (the village) and *yama* (the mountain) are at the heart of the community's existence in the countryside, where it is especially important to balance the need for modern conveniences with the traditional way of life. Shown here are scenes from the Aizu region in Fukushima (top photo) and Asuka Village in Nara (bottom photo). Japanese government agencies, non-profit organizations and the United Nations University are collaborating to promote the merits of *satoyama* to the rest of the world. The aim is to seek solutions through socio-ecological initiatives. Read more about the Satoyama Initiative at the following links:

- **Satoyama Initiative** https://satoyama-initiative.org/about/
- **Greetings from Satoyama** https://ourworld.unu.edu/en/greetings-from-satoyama

4
Shikoku & Kyushu

TO SEE MORE FROM CHAPTER 4,
SCAN THIS QR CODE

Sanuki Fuji
Kagawa

Mt. Iino is the pride and joy of the locals. It is believed to be as beautiful as Mt. Fuji, and it is affectionately called Sanuki Fuji. Everywhere in Japan, there are beautiful mounts with references to Mt. Fuji. Several good examples can be found in this book: Mt. Bandai (P18) is known as Aizu Fuji; Mt. Yotei (P25) is known as Ezo Fuji; Mt. Daisen (P52) is called Izumo Fuji; Sakurajima (P75) is referred to as Chikushi Fuji.

Mt. Fuji is dear in the hearts of the Japanese. Japan's premiere mount is symbolic of a number of things, ranging from hopes and dreams on a personal level to a commonly shared love for the land and nature. It is easy to understand why a replica should exist in the backyard. (By the same token, most towns seem to have a shopping street named The Ginza!)

Mornings are calm around Sanuki Fuji. Face it from Miyaike to see a clear mirror image reflected on the water's surface. The gentle slope looks sweet, like something out of an *anime* movie. The slightly tapered shape and the ponds at the base of the mountain are part of the unique features found in the Sanuki Plains.

GETTING THERE To climb Mt. Iino, take the Community Bus (Iino/Nakatsu Route) for Iinoyama Tozan-guchi bus stop from Marugame train station. Mt. Iino is 400m above sea level. The hike takes about an hour on established trails.

Shimanto River

Kochi

The Japanese like to group things in threes, like the three best, or the three biggest, or the top three in any category. Not surprisingly, even the clarity of water flowing through streams and rivers get grouped into Japan's three most clear-flowing rivers. Shimanto River is one of those, spanning through Kochi Prefecture for 196 kilometers. The other two rivers in this category are the Nagara River (Gifu) and Kakita River (Shizuoka).

At its most upstream location in Nakasato-cho, in the Onomi district, a concrete bridge that was built in the late 1950s does more than connect opposite sides of the river. Naro Bridge is a gathering place. Late in the afternoons, people start to congregate toward the benches in the middle of the bridge. It is time to socialize, and soon they become engrossed in a long conversation. Their daily walks take them to a spot where they can connect with friends, old and new. Getting permission to take their picture can even spark new friendships.

Surrounded by the mountain forests, this tranquil village has crystal clear waters flowing through it, and fresh clean air to fill the lungs. Maybe these are the secrets to longevity. On summer nights, tiny little lights spark across the water and beyond, as far away as the rice paddies that stretch out on both sides of the river. Fireflies are dancing about.

GETTING THERE 20 minutes from Tosakure train station by taxi.

Ochiai Village
Tokushima

Far into the mountainous region of Tokushima, Ouboke Gorge and the Iya Kazura-bashi are two scenic landmarks in the central Iya region. Further into the hills, Ochiai Village is like most places in Japan where the scenery remains unblemished: it is a hideaway.

    Negotiating the winding riverside road is not easy on the way to the Ochiai Village Observation Point. From the opposite side of the hamlet, the houses look as if they are desperately hanging on to the side of the hill. If you get there at dawn after the rain, the mist rises from the valley and weaves around, moving up and down, fluctuating, thinning out here, thickening there. Lights from the village peek through the fog to add wonderment to the scene.

    There are a few villages in Shikoku where the houses are built on a steep slope, but Ochiai is especially amazing.

Hakata Island

Ehime

In the southwest corner of Japan lies the smallest of the main islands, Shikoku. Taking up more than a third on the west side of Shikoku is Ehime Prefecture. Off the coast of Ehime, a few of the small islands in the Seto Inland Sea belong to Imaji city. One of them is called Hakata Island. It sounds like the city in Fukuoka, but the *kanji* spelling is not the same, and this place definitely has a mark of its own.

Try approaching from Hiroshima. You will go across a series of bridges known as the Shimanami Kaido (Nishiseto Expressway) to arrive in Imabari on the Ehime side. The crossing is an island hopping experience. Not only is the bridge an architectural marvel, the breathtaking scenery along the way is superb. The scenic route is about 60 kilometers long for cars, and 70 kilometers for the separate path for pedestrians and bicycles. If you are looking for a great outdoor experience, join the ranks of tourists from all over the world and take the bike route.

TRAVEL NOTES

| **Imabari / Kurushima Strait** | Itoyama Park in Imabari is worth a stop. The lighthouse there is a vantage point for views of Kurushima Strait and the islands. At night, lights from passing ships drift slowly across the darkness. The lone bright light shining amid the linear effect belongs to the lighthouse, a beacon in the dark for all ships big and small.

GETTING THERE To see the lighthouse, take the bus from Imabari train station for a 20-minute ride to the Tenbodai Iriguchi bus stop. Itoyama Park is a 10-minute walk.

GETTING THERE From Imabari, Hiroshima or Fukuyama train station, take the Shimanami Liner highway bus for Hakata Bus Center, then 10 minutes by car.
• **Tourist information** http://www.go-shimanami.jp/global/english/

 KYUSHU

Yame Tea Fields
Fukuoka

The Yame Central Tea Garden is a plantation situated on gentle slopes. Tea harvested in this area is of the highest quality. The best tea from Fukuoka—in taste, fragrance and color—is sold as *Yame cha* (Yame tea).

The Tea Garden is open to visitors. You can follow the private farm roads within the plantation to the observation area. On a clear day, you can see all the way to the Ariake Sea. The fields of green spread out before your eyes, the beauty of the land pronounced by symmetry and lazy curves. The poles standing in the fields are wind machines. The large fan blades help circulate the air and protect the crops from frost. Natural breezes flow through as well. The gentle puffs seem to send word that *shincha*, the first harvest, is ready. *Yame cha* is sold in the outlet store inside the Tea Garden.

GETTING THERE From Hainuzuka train station, a car ride will take 20 minutes to the Yame Central Tea Garden.

Hiraodai

Fukuoka

A small rural town thrives at the base of the Hiraodai Limestone Plateau. After driving through rice paddies, the road starts its ascent. At the top of the hill, a panoramic vista of rolling plains hits the sky. It is an open view but the plains are not bare. They are embellished with limestone rock formations, as if a fistful of boulders were dropped from the sky and scattered upon the grassy fields. The karst formation at Hiraodai can look like a herd of sheep, and that is how this area got its name of *Yogunbaru* (Fields of Sheep).

Take a nature walk and see if you can make out some of the interesting shapes like Kissing Rocks and Gutsy Tree. The caves underground are a feature of karst topography. A number of them are open to the public, like Senbutsu Cave and Mejiro Limestone Cave. Stop at the Nature Observation Center before venturing off to explore the area. Hiraodai is one of Japan's three great karst landscapes. The other two are Akiyoshidai Plateau (Yamaguchi) and Shikoku Karst Natural Park (Kochi-Ehime).

GETTING THERE 20 minutes by car from Ishiharamachi train station.
• Kitakyushu City Tourism Information http://www.gururich-kitaq.com/en/

Chikugo River Drawbridge

Saga

At the mouth of the Chikugo River is a drawbridge called Shokai-kyo. It connects Fukuoka and Saga. Previously used exclusively for rail transport, today it is a pedestrian bridge that is lowered eight times a day so people can cross on foot. The bridge has an industrial silhouette. Photographers like to take its profile in the sunset, moving with the sun, following the sun's directional angle. If the clouds stay out of the way, the shots turn out better than expected. At night, the bridge is outlined in colorful blinking lights, alternating every few seconds from red to blue and different colors. The hypnotic motion of the changing lights might hold you captive for a while.

GETTING THERE In Fukuoka: from Nishitetsu Yanagawa train station, take the bus for Saga train station to Okawa-bashi bus stop, about a 25-minute ride. The drawbridge is a 10-minute walk. In Saga: from Saga train station, 25 minutes by city bus to Shokai-kyo bus stop. The drawbridge is a 5-minute walk.
• Saga Official Travel Guide https://www.saga-tripgenius.com/

VENTURING OUT

| **Tara / The Submarine Road** | The tide can cause some interesting things to appear in the Ariake Sea, where the ebb and flow can drastically change sea levels by as much as six meters. At low tide, the road in Tara-cho is passable. In high tide, the road gets swallowed up by seawater. It is a submarine road that runs along the rocky shoreline and into the sea. Countless support posts stand straight out of the water. These are used for seaweed farming. Near the road is also a *torii* that seems to rise and fall with the tide.

Working the rough seas can be a tough way to earn a living. Battered by the crashing waves, the weathered roads and telephone poles in this seaside community have withstood the test of time. The unwavering posture of determined people has supported both the infrastructure and the traditions of maritime culture.

Kujuku Islands
Nagasaki

A ria formation created more than 200 small islands in Sasebo. No one really counted the number of isles before naming them the *Kujuku-shima* (Ninety-nine Islands) in this northwest part of Kyushu; 99 just seemed like a big enough number to include all of them on the coastline of Nagasaki.

Sasebo city has several good viewing spots, like Ishidake and Funakoshi observatories, complete with walking paths and ample parking. This photo was taken from Ishidake Observatory. (The Last Samurai was filmed here.) A short walk along the footpath from the parking lot toward the forest reveals a wide open vista that is utterly remarkable. The ocean is true blue during the day, while the evening sun turns the water a bright red. Cruise ships weave through the isles and leave a long white foamy trail behind in their wake. Ah, the open seas are vast.

GETTING THERE 15 minutes by car from Sasebo train station to the Ishidake Observatory. To reach Kujuku Islands, take the city bus from Sasebo train station. The Kujukushima Pearl Sea Resort has an aquarium, restaurants, shops, water sports facilities and day cruises. • **Visit Nagasaki** https://visit-nagasaki.com/spots/detail/222

WHY IT'S SPECIAL

▸▸ Preserving the Harvest

There are many ways to make the fresh harvest last longer than its shelf life, like freezing, canning, dehydrating, candying, pickling and more. In Japan, sun dried fruits, pickled vegetables and candied goods are common. Fermentation is another frequently used preservation method for *miso* paste and *natto* soybeans. Pickled vegetables are condiments that accompany almost every meal, like the *daikon* radishes made into *takuan* on P13. In colder climates, vegetables and even *tofu* are stored outside to freeze in the natural elements. Candying can be dry as in *amanatto* (sweet beans), or wet as in *kanro* (syrup) chestnuts.

Fall is the season for stringing persimmons together to hang from the eaves where there is good ventilation. The top photo shows *hoshigaki* (dried persimmons) being air dried on a farm in Yamanashi, where the treat is locally known as *korogaki* (aged and frosted persimmons). After several weeks, the sweet flavor gets enhanced in the ripening process and a natural sugar coating will form on the skin of the fruit. Unlike other dried fruits, moist and gummy persimmons are tastier. They will go to market in the yellow crates when the texture is just right.

In the other photo, *umeboshi* (dried plums) that were first packed in salt are now being sun dried in the yard at a farmhouse in Niigata. Red *shiso* leaves (perilla or crispa, a type of Japanese basil) are added for color and mild zesty flavor.

Food preservation is no longer limited to farm work as dehydration and pickling gain popularity in home kitchens. Recipes for some of the preserved foods introduced here can be found readily on the internet. Sample them during your travels, then try your hand at making something when you return home!

Aso
Kumamoto

Rolling hills and beautiful greenery are the first impressions of summer in Aso. This view is from the mysterious Oshitoishi Hill, where gigantic boulders sit on a grassy knoll. The 360-degree panoramic view from the hilltop is dramatic.

The breeze will feel good. Plant your bare feet in the grass and gaze into the distance for a

GETTING THERE Aso is a large tourist area served by six train stations; among them Uchinomaki, Aso and Takimizu. To visit Oshitoishi Hill: 40 minutes by car from Aso train station. • **Aso Tourism Portal Site** http://www.asocity-kanko.jp/en/top/

while. The Aso mountain range will stare back. In the fall, the fields turn golden.

These pastures here have been tended for hundreds of years. The fields are burned in the spring for pest control and overgrowth management. If you have yet to witness a prescribed burn, watch how they are conducted on a grand scale here.

Nagasakibana

Oita

Nagasakibana is a point on the northern tip of the Kunisaki Peninsula, famous for *nanohana* (canola flowers) covering the entire area with bright yellow blooms in spring. Terraced fields overflowing with seasonal plantings create an image that could be straight out of a song that Japanese children sing in school. Sunflowers dominate the fields in the summer.

You can go swimming, you can go camping, you can play in the sun. At Matama Beach, wavy stripes are left in the sand as the tide goes out. Uneven peaks in the rocky cliffs rise into a majestic mountainscape. There are so many sights to see in Kunisaki: temples, shrines, castles, manors and even Japan's version of Machu Picchu in Usa, adding noteworthy cultural interest to outdoor fun.

GETTING THERE 40 minutes by Oita Kotsu bus from Usa train station to Nagasakibana Kyanpujo Iriguchi bus stop.

VENTURING OUT

| **Yufuin** | Oita is called Onsen Prefecture because there are so many hot springs. Beppu might be the most famous one, but when it comes to scenic views, Yufuin tops them all. The gentle slopes of Mount Yufu, the clear waters of Yufu River meandering through the fields, *onsen* towns, Kinrin Lake, railroads—the list is long.

Yufuin lies in a basin. After the rain, and especially after a night of radiative cooling, the whole town is covered in a blanket of fog. A great spot to take in this vista is at Jakoshi Pass along the Yamanami Highway. The drive up the winding mountain road is rewarding.

Seasonal changes give Yufuin many faces. In the spring, when cherry trees and *nanohana* bloom together on the banks of Yufu River, photographers overrun the place. Lots of good subjects to focus on, like shots toward the mountains from the riverbanks or a close-up of the rails. A visit to Yufuin the old-fashioned way could be fun aboard the restored vintage train called *Yufuin no Mori*. Eat, shop, and browse the arts too.

GETTING THERE 10-minute walk from Yufuin train station to the banks of Yufu River.

Takachiho

Miyazaki

Takachiho should be at the top of the list of every Kyushu itinerary. The gorge is another miracle of nature, with its vertical rock formations surrounding the steep crevices that drop to the Gokase River. The best views are from the rowboats. Get close to the Manai Waterfall and feel the roaring waters reverberate. You might even think the background humming is a song of ancient myths and legends. If you are inclined to stay on the ground, there is a trail that leads to a viewing point on the opposite side of the waterfall. Here you can see the entire cascade.

Nearby Kunimigaoka is famous for a sea of clouds. You can drive all the way up to the observation point. Both the parking lot and promenade provide a safe perch even in dim light. The best time of year to see the white blanket is in the fall, when temperatures are low and the air is still. A sea of clouds will form when the skies clear up after the rain, but even if the conditions are not perfect for a full "sea" to develop, a dreamy landscape can still materialize in the fog.

GETTING THERE 15 minutes by car from the Takachiho Bus Center.
• **Takachiho Tourist Association** http://takachiho-kanko.info/en/

Sakurajima

Kagoshima

One of the iconic landscapes of Kagoshima Prefecture is a former island. Years ago, Sakurajima was actually a separate land mass. Today it is contiguous with the rest of Kyushu, the result of molten rock filling the channel when Sakurajima erupted in 1914. It is still an active volcano, repeatedly spewing lava and ashes around it.

Best known as the birthplace of Saigo Takamori, an influential leader of the Meiji Restoration during the late 19th Century, Sakurajima is a uniquely rich land full of history, a distinctive culture and delectable dishes. About those local goodies: *shirokuma* is a sweet treat of creamy shaved ice topped with candies and fruits like jewelry tossed on snow. You have to try it.

GETTING THERE From Kagoshima, 15 minutes by ferry from the Sakurajima Ferry Terminal or 70 minutes by bus from Kagoshima Airport to Sakurajima-guchi bus stop. *This view: Satsuma Bay side of Tarumi City.*
● Kagoshima Tourism http://www.kagoshima-kankou.com/for/

WHY IT'S SPECIAL

▸▸ Zekkei

Amazing, gorgeous, outstanding, superb, wondrous. How many words can describe the incredible views you can see only in Japan? There is a word for it in Japanese—*zekkei*—that an English translation cannot fully capture. Here are a few wonderland sites in Japan to put on your bucket list. See more at

● **Zekkei Japan** https://zekkeijapan.com
(in six languages)

Amaharashi Coast (Toyama)

Miyako Island viewed from Kurima Island (Okinawa)

5
Good
To
Know

TO SEE MORE FROM CHAPTER 5,
SCAN THIS QR CODE

In the Countryside

Just as good manners are welcome everywhere in the world, special consideration should be given in the Japanese countryside.

Greetings with a smile
Ohayo(gozaimasu) ············ Good morning
(add the formal ending to address elders)
Konnichiwa ············ Hello (day greeting)
Konbanwa ············ Hello (evening greeting)
Arigato(gozaimasu) ············ Thank you
(add the formal ending to address elders)
Doitashimashite ············ You're welcome
(*domo* works, casually)
Domo ············ Thanks, casually
Dozo ············ Please, casually

Keep yen on hand
Be sure to have enough cash to pay for your expenses in rural areas. Many shops and restaurants do not accept credit cards. Not all regional banks can exchange foreign currency, and not all ATMs can recognize credit cards registered outside Japan. Exchange yen while you are in metropolitan areas.

At the *ryokan*
Charges for a stay at the *ryokan*, the traditional Japanese style inn, are generally per person and not per room. A stay usually includes a sumptuous dinner and a Japanese style breakfast. Confirm whether the *ryokan* charges per person or per room when you make reservations, and whether meals are included.

Be mindful of those around you
Try not to draw attention. Keep your hands to yourself, keep down the noise, and keep your belongings close. As ambassadors, let us conduct ourselves at all times in a manner which our fellow countrymen would be proud.

No spitting, no trashing
Do not spit, including gum. If you need to rid of something from your mouth (this includes untasty food) wrap it in a napkin or a piece of paper and dispose it in a trash can. If you are in a restaurant, place it on the table to be cleared away. Do not throw rubbish on the street; find a trash receptacle.

Modesty is appreciated
Dress modestly and try not to show too much skin. Unless you are swimming, wear more than a bathing suit.

No tipping necessary
There is no custom of tipping for services rendered in Japan. Do not add a tip to your final bill, but a quick *arigato* and a smile will go a long way.

Public restrooms
If you need to use the toilet, look for the nearest train station, convenience store or gas station. Most are equipped with public restrooms. Ask to use the facilities at convenience stores and gas stations, but the ones at the train stations are accessible to the public. Carry some tissue or hand wipes at all times, just in case.

Early morning views
Some of the most beautiful landscapes are in the morning light before 10:00 AM. There are fewer tourists early in the day, too, so try to rise early.

No trespassing
When the townscape is part of the tourist area, some homes are open to the public. But most homes are not. Do not enter private residences. Keep out!

Stay off private property
Open pastures may not be fenced, but that does not mean they are open to the public. Do not enter fields that belong to private farms where livestock graze although the grass and landscape look tempting. The same goes for the narrow footpaths that farmers use for accessing the rice paddies.

Drink local
There are many famous springs in Japan: *Kyougoku* in Hokkaido, *Ryugakubo* in Niigata, *Oike Yusuigun* in Oita, *Hakushuu* in Yamanashi. These are among the *meisui* (famous spring water) that can be enjoyed during your visit. Convenience stores (*conbini*) and grocery stores carry bottled spring water, and rest stops along toll roads also have their *meisui* version. Check out the link below for a list of Japan's *meisui*. In addition to spring water, each region has its own local brew of *sake* and *shochu*. See Japan's 100 Remarkable Waters at:
https://www.mizuhiroba.jp/en/meisui/

Eat local
Japan is a land of four seasons with bountiful harvests from the earth as well as the sea. Each region boasts a local delicacy in season. Ask for what is *shun* (of the moment) and experience the local cuisine. Many dishes are served only in that part of the country, so take advantage of your visit. Japan's cost of living might be high, but food is quite reasonably priced.

Roadside markets
In fishing and farming communities, local produce is sold in fresh markets. About 20 years ago, roadside facilities were established in remote areas for the convenience of residents and visitors. Today there are about a thousand or so *michi-no-eki* (roadside stations) located throughout Japan. Look for souvenirs and grab a quick bite to eat at a *michi-no-eki* near your travels. For locations throughout Japan, see https://www.michi-no-eki.jp/stations/english

Water or tea, anyone?
There is no charge for water served in Japanese restaurants, eateries and coffee shops. The water may come from the tap, but potable water runs throughout Japan so it is safe to drink unless otherwise posted. If you prefer no ice, just say, "No ice please." In some places, *ocha* (green tea) is served after the meal; also complimentary. *Ocha* might be cold in summer, hot in winter. If you ask for iced tea, it might be a menu item and you will be charged.

Izakaya, the Japanese pub
When you are seated at a restaurant, you will be provided with a hot or cold towel (depending on the season) to freshen up. Place the used towel back in its basket or tray. At the *izakaya*, a Japanese style pub, you will also be served a small dish called *otoushi* or *tsukidashi* before you place your order. This is a form of table charge that usually runs around 500 yen. If you want no surprises on your final bill, ask in advance how much you will be charged for the *otoushi* when it is served.

Trash, garbage, refuse and rubbish
Recycling is a conscientious effort throughout Japan, and throwing things away can be a complicated maneuver. Trash is divided into things that will burn and things that won't burn. Recyclables are divided into paper, plastic, glass and tins. Receptacles are color-coded and/or labeled accordingly. Graphics will help identify the correct container in most cases. Train stations are equipped with receptacles. Japan welcomes your kind cooperation to keep this corner of Earth clutter-free.

Don't touch the trash
Furniture and large household items sitting by the curb are not free for the taking! Do not be tempted to rummage through them, either. Japan has a regulated disposal system for getting rid of *sodai gomi* (oversized refuse). Residents must first reserve a pick-up date, then pay a disposal fee by purchasing a sticker of pre-designated value according to the item. The oversized item placed at the curb has the paid sticker and the disposer's name. Someone else's trash is not your treasure. It is still private property. Do not touch!

Sssshhhh we're sleeping
In rural areas, most people head home at dusk to relax with their families. Nights are quiet and activities are minimal. There is no night life, so do not start one with your own party.

References Online

Here are a few select websites from the Editor to help you prepare for your trip to Japan. URL addresses are current as of January 2019.

GENERAL INFORMATION

Japan Official Travel App: First things first: Get JNTO's free app for comprehensive, on-time information to travel safely and comfortably throughout Japan. In English, Chinese and Korean.
https://www.jnto.go.jp/smartapp/eng/

Visiting Japan: Ministry of Foreign Affairs government website in 43 languages.
https://www.mofa.go.jp/link/visit.html

Japan Tourism Agency: Press releases and in-depth articles from the Ministry of Land, Infrastructure, Transport and Tourism. Good academic stuff to study before you go.
http://www.mlit.go.jp/kankocho/en/

Japan National Tourism Organization (JNTO): Japan's official tourism website provides comprehensive travel information in multiple languages. Scroll to the very bottom for language settings.
https://www.japan.travel/en/

Newsletters: JNTO's page where you can sign up for newsletters in your native language.
https://www.japan.travel/en/contact/

Tourist Information Centers: JNTO's list of tourist information centers that can assist foreign travelers in English and other languages.
https://tic.jnto.go.jp/

Enjoy My Japan: More about Japan from JNTO in English, German and French.
https://www.enjoymyjapan.jp/

Visit! National Park: Ministry of Environment's official guide to national parks in English and Japanese.
http://www.env.go.jp/en/nature/enjoy-project/

National Parks of Japan: General information provided by Ministry of Environment in English and Japanese.
https://www.env.go.jp/park/

Japan I Can: Online bookings managed by Japan's largest and prestigious Japan Travel Bureau (JTB). Change language settings from the top of the screen.
https://www.japanican.com/en/

DiGJAPAN: Multilingual travel app with coupons and useful information. Change language settings at the top of the screen.
http://www.mapple.co.jp/digjapan/en/

Japan Guide: Plan your trip by destination or by interest in English and Chinese. Scroll down to the very bottom to change language settings.
http://www.japan-guide.com/

Japan Travel: Multilingual travel agency offering a range of services from group tours to personal concierge. Articles sharing experiences are written by travelers like you. Select language from top right of screen.
https://en.japantravel.com

Boutique Japan: Boutique-style agency founded by transplanted New Yorker specializing in personalized tours. Guide "ninjas" from different countries currently live in Japan. In English.
https://boutiquejapan.com/

Luggage-free Travel: Have someone else transport your luggage within Japan while you travel. Book online. Select language from top right of screen.
https://www.luggage-free-travel.com/

Savor Japan: Restaurant guide searchable by area; information on Japanese cuisine, types of food, table etiquette, chefs. In English, Chinese, Korean, Japanese.
https://savorjapan.com/

Hitou (Secret Springs): Guide to secluded hot springs and hideaways compiled by (none other than) the Japan Association of Secluded Hot Spring Inns. Search by area and make reservations online in English or Japanese.
http://www.hitou.or.jp/en/

Kyoto Private Tours: Tour Kyoto in a private car with an English-speaking chauffeur.

http://privatetour-kyoto.com/ehome.htm

TRANSPORTATION AND NAVIGATION

Japan Transit Planner: Search train routes, transfer points and routing options, Rail Pass and Tokyo Subway Ticket information. Select from 13 languages under SETTING & LANGUAGE.
https://world.jorudan.co.jp/mln/en/

HyperDia: Train and bus navigation site with timetables and schedules. Search by date, time, departure and destination points. In Japanese, English, Chinese.
http://www.hyperdia.com/en/

NAVITIME Japan Journey Planner: Plan your travel routing by train, bus, car, airline, or walking tours. For PCs, also available as an app and in 18 languages. Set your preference from top right of page.
https://transit.navitime.com/en/jp/

NAVITIME for Japan Travel: Quick link to navigation app for English users. Do spot searches, plan route options, read travel guides. Compatible with iOS and Android. Also available in 17 other languages.
https://www.navitime.co.jp/pcstorage/html/japan_travel/english/

Japan Direct: Free app for iOS users to find the best train route.
https://itunes.apple.com/us/app/japan-direct-route-and-train/id1383391252?mt=8

Traffic Safety: Must-read information on rules of the road in Japan, traffic safety and tips for tourists provided by the Tokyo Metropolitan Police Department in multiple languages. Click on MULTILINGUAL at the top of the page to select language preference.
http://www.keishicho.metro.tokyo.jp/multilingual/english/traffic_safety/traffic_rules/

MOBILE PHONES

Haneda Airport: Rental locations at Haneda Airport.
http://www.haneda-tokyo-access.com/en/wingairport/service.html

Narita Airport: Rental locations at Narita Airport.
https://www.narita-airport.jp/en/service/svc_19

EMERGENCY CONTACTS

Japan Visitor / Telephone Numbers: A list of important phone numbers for travelers, courtesy of Japan Air Lines.
https://www.japanvisitor.com/japan-travel/trav-telephone-number

NHK World News: NHK, Japan's public television, streams news and programs online in English. In the event of an emergency, NHK World will provide updates in 18 languages. Also available as an app.
https://www3.nhk.or.jp/nhkworld/

Police Information: How to contact local police and tips for tourists provided by the Tokyo Metropolitan Police Department in multiple languages. Click on MULTILINGUAL at the top of the page to select language preference.
http://www.keishicho.metro.tokyo.jp/multilingual/english/

MEDICAL EMERGENCY NUMBERS

Hospital Information
Tokyo 03 3212 2323

Metropolitan Medical & Health
Info Center (M-F 9-8) 03 5285 8181

International Medical Information Center
Tokyo (M-F 9-5, Sa 10-1) 03 5285 8088
Osaka (M-F 10-5) 06 4395 0555

Modes of Transportation

Go North to South, East to West, cross-country and zig zag around. No matter where your starting point, final destination or stops in between might take you, the transportation system in Japan is one of the best in the world.

On the Trains

Trains are a convenient way to travel throughout Japan. JR lines and privately owned railways run from urban centers to the suburbs and rural areas, while subway systems in major cities provide fast transport. By making the right connections within the public transportation system, almost every corner of Japan is accessible.

About the train system

Japan's rail transport system is operated primarily by JR (formerly state-owned) and other privately owned and operated railway companies (*shitetsu* or *mintetsu*). JR has a nationwide network, while the privately owned railways are regionally based. *Shitetsu* or *mintetsu* is usually translated as "private railway," but that does not mean the trains are for private use only. They are part of the public transportation system. JR was a state-owned railway system called *kokutetsu* (national railways) until it was privatized in the 1980s. The distinction between the JR system and the ones run by privately owned companies continue today.

To board any train — JR or otherwise — a fare ticket must be purchased and validated at the ticket booth. Ticket booths can be automated or manned by a conductor. Fares depend on the destination, calculated by the distance covered. The fare ticket will be collected at the destination as you exit the station through the ticket booth. You can purchase fare tickets each time you ride the trains, or invest in a pre-paid and rechargeable smart card, called IC Cards. To use an IC Card, tap it against the sensor at the automated ticket booth when you enter and exit the train station. The fare for that segment of travel will be deducted from the total amount that is already credited on the IC Card (see below).

How to ride the trains

Good information on how to use the passenger rail system in Japan is available online from two informative websites. Go to Japan-Guide's "Taking the Train in Japan" page (scroll all the way down to select English or Chinese from the bottom right of the screen) or West Japan Railway Company's FAQ sheets (in English) from the links below.
https://www.japan-guide.com/e/e2016.html
http://www.westjr.co.jp/global/en/howto/wjr_faq.pdf

Privately owned railways

Sixteen major railway corporations operate in Japan, along with 50 smaller privately owned rail companies that are locally based. From Japan Private Railway Association's website, learn more about *mintetsu* (short for *minkan tetsudo*, or private sector railways). Click on each region to see which companies operate in that area, then click again on one of the railways for more information on where to go and what to see along their routes. The website is well organized and thorough enough to plan your entire rail travel by *mintetsu*. Select from eight languages from GLOBAL SITE at the top right of the page.
https://www.mintetsu.or.jp/en/

Metro

In Tokyo, Osaka, Nagoya, Kyoto, Sapporo, Fukuoka and other metropolitan areas, the metro is a well-developed subway network within the city. Some metro lines connect directly to the outlying suburban areas and beyond. See Japan Subway Association's website for a nationwide directory of Japan's underground rail system. Click on WORLD PLAZA at the top right of the screen to set your language preference in English, Chinese, Korean or Japanese.
http://www.jametro.or.jp/en/

Prepaid fare cards (IC Cards)

If you have one of the ten major fare cards, you can use it on almost all trains, subways and buses. These prepaid cards are compatible for use in most cities, so if you purchase one prepaid fare card, you won't have to purchase a ticket each time you ride the train or bus. Fare cards are prepaid and rechargeable. Time is always precious, especially when you are travelling, so why not invest in the convenience? The article prepared by Japan-Guide is an excellent source of information.

Japan Rail Pass
If you plan to ride the bullet train, JR's Japan Rail Pass is the best deal around. With a few exceptions, the pass is good for limitless travel on railways operated by the six JR companies, most bullet trains and even buses. It's an all-you-can-ride buffet pass, valid for a choice of seven, 14 or 21 days. You can also choose from first class Green Cars or open seating in Ordinary Cars. Purchase an Exchange Order from an authorized agent before you leave home, then go to one of the JR ticket offices shown on the link below to turn in your Exchange Order for a pass. In addition to the nationwide travel opportunity made possible by Japan Rail Pass, regional passes are also available. Read more at the link below.
For general information and list of authorized agents overseas:
http://japanrailpass.net/en/about_jrp.html
For JR exchange offices in Japan:
http://www.japanrailpass.net/en/exchange.html

Kansai Thru Pass
Unlimited local travel on subways, *mintetsu* and buses throughout the Kansai area is made possible by the Kansai Thru Pass. You can go all over the Osaka Bay area and into parts north of Kyoto using a combination of trains and buses. Choose from 2-day or 3-day options. Some restrictions apply. Click on the map at the left of the page from the link below for specific stops. In English, Chinese, Korean, Thai and Japanese. Set language preference from top of page.
http://www.surutto.com/tickets/kansai_thru_english.html

More passes
The Kakuyasu Ryoko (Budget Travel) Company has compiled discounted passes as an exclusive service to visiting tourists. The company is still working on updating their English language website, but essential information is well organized as of this writing. From their website, click on the type of pass that interests you, and it will link to detailed information on what the pass will cover and where to buy it. Someone has done the research for you so all you have to do is choose where you want to go and how much you want to save. In English and Japanese.
https://en.kakuyasu-ryoko.com/tickets/exclusive-rail-passes-and-tickets

By Air
Japan has a surprising number of airports served by the two major airlines and other low cost carriers and regional airlines within its small geographical area. Practically every prefecture has a regional airport, so hopping through Japan in short flight segments can cover a large area within your limited time in Japan.

ANA and JAL
Both major airlines, All Nippon Airways (ANA) and Japan Air Lines (JAL), offer domestic flights. Discounted airfares for foreign travelers are a good deal indeed at 5,000~10,000 yen between destinations for one-way travel. If you need to fly long distances, take advantage of the big savings from ANA's JAPAN Fare and JAL's Japan Explorer Pass. You can purchase both discounted airfare passes in advance or after arriving in country.
https://www.ana.co.jp/en/us/promotions/share/experience_jp/
http://www.world.jal.co.jp/world/en/japan_explorer_pass/lp/

Jetstar
Connect from China, Indonesia, Malaysia, New Zealand, Philippines, Singapore, Thailand, Vietnam and multiple points in Australia into 15 regional airports in Japan.
https://www.jetstar.com/au/en/home

Air Asia
From major cities in Asia, fly to Narita, Haneda, Kansai and Fukuoka.
https://www.airasia.com/booking/home/en/gb

Skymark Airlines
From Hokkaido to Okinawa, this domestic carrier flies between 11 regional airports.
http://www.skymark.co.jp/en/

Peach Aviation and Vanilla Air
Low cost carriers of the ANA group fly to and from Narita, Kansai, Shin Chitose, Shanghai and Hong Kong.
https://www.flypeach.com/jp
https://www.vanilla-air.com/en/

Air Do
Fly to Hokkaido's six airports from Sendai, Haneda or Nagoya. Foreign passport holders are eligible for deep discounts.
https://www.airdo.jp/en/

Solaseed Air
The Kyushu-based carrier flies between

Kyushu and Okinawa to Haneda, Kobe and central Japan.
https://www.solaseedair.jp/en/

On the Bus

Although traffic congestion can get heavy in urban areas and highways during peak travel periods, buses can be an inexpensive choice of public transportation for sightseeing in Japan.

Long distance buses
Highway buses cover long distances, many of them offering night departures so you can reach your destination in the morning. Several bus lines operate throughout Japan and offer online booking in multiple languages.

Japan Bus-Gateway
This highway bus information platform presented by the Ministry of Land, Infrastructure, Transport and Tourism is a comprehensive guide to long distance buses operating in Japan, complete with a search tool and reservation system. In English, Chinese, Korean and Japanese.
https://highway-bus.jnto.go.jp/en/

Japan Bus Online
Japan's largest booking website for bus travel covers over 200 routes by 93 bus companies. User friendly search tool and useful travel information in English, Chinese and Japanese.
https://japanbusonline.com/en

Japan Bus Lines (JBL)
Purchase a bus pass good for 3 days, 5 days or 7 days of unlimited travel on express buses running on 93 different routes. Passes are valid for 60 days from the purchase date. In English, Chinese, Korean and Japanese.
http://japanbuslines.com/en/buspass/

Local buses
Inner city bus lines cover an extensive network of scheduled routes and stops. Buses run on a surprisingly reliable timetable in spite of traffic. Timetables are posted at the bus stop. As with trains, buses might run on different times on Sundays and holidays and are usually printed in red on the timetable. Bus fares can be paid in cash or by using a prepaid fare card (IC Cards). Fares can depend on the distance travelled, and although they are usually posted inside the bus in Japanese, using a prepaid fare card would be much easier than to query the bus driver about the fare. For information on how to ride the bus, see the link below to Japan-Guide's Transportation page.
https://www.japan-guide.com/e/e2015.html

One-day bus passes
Some bus lines offer a one-day pass for unlimited rides. Check with your hotel to see if the local bus line offers day passes.
For Tokyo Toei Bus lines (in 6 languages)
https://www.kotsu.metro.tokyo.jp/eng/tickets/value.html
For Nagoya City Bus (in 9 languages)
https://www.kotsu.city.nagoya.jp/en/pc/TICKET/TRP0001071.htm
For Kyoto City Bus (in 5 languages)
https://www2.city.kyoto.lg.jp/kotsu/webguide/en/ticket/regular_1day_card_bus.html
For Fukuoka City Bus (in 5 languages)
http://www.nishitetsu.jp/en/ticket/

Community buses
Smaller towns in outlying areas provide community buses and shuttle services for area residents as an alternate mode of transportation. The community buses servicing suburban and rural communities make it possible to reach places where trains do not run. This is also a convenient way for tourists to get around and costs only about 100 yen per ride. If the town you want to explore has a community bus, it will most likely start at the local train station. Hop on and off to see the sights along the way, then circle back to the train station. Be sure to check the timetable for the last bus!

By Taxi

Taxi and car services in Japan are licensed by the government. Flat rate airport transfers are available, taxis run on a meter, and private car tours are always an ideal option.

Taxis in general
Flagging down a taxi is easy in metropolitan areas of Japan. Major terminals and most train stations will have a taxi stand. The custom in Japan is to line up in an orderly fashion for almost everything, so be polite. In rural and remote areas, taxis are on call. Information should be available from your place of stay, so be sure to carry the phone number of the local taxi service while you are out and about.

Airport transfers
from Haneda and Narita Airports
Friends and families traveling in small groups of 3 or 4 might find flat rate airport transfers to be convenient and economical compared to

airport shuttle services or trains.
https://hinomaru.tokyo/airport?locale=en

Private car tours
From Tokyo and Yokohama to outlying areas such as Mt. Fuji and Yamanashi, consider a private tour by car with a driver/guide.
https://hinomaru.tokyo/daytrip-taxi

Osaka International Visitors Taxi
Taxi service is available in English, Chinese and Korean for tourists visiting the Kansai Area including Osaka, Kyoto, Nara, Kobe.
https://www.osaka-int-taxi-eng.com/

Kyoto Foreign Friendly Taxi Service
Two taxi stands in Kyoto are dedicated to foreign passengers who need English-speaking drivers. Some drivers also speak other foreign languages. Download the app in English, Chinese or Korean.
https://kyoto.travel/files/ff-taxi.pdf

Tottori Tourist Taxi
Tottori City is offering a 3-hour tourist taxi at a flat rate of 2,000 yen for a limited time. Drivers speak English, Chinese or Korean. The service offers suggested itineraries to see the sand dunes and the San'in Coast.
http://www.city.tottori.lg.jp/www/contents/1374222847656/index.html

By Bicycle

Very popular today is the option to tour Japan by bicycle. People of all ages ride bikes in Japan on a daily basis, and some of the world's best models are made in Japan. Serious cyclists can bring their own collapsible bikes with check-in luggage, but getting around Japan on public transportation with your bike can be a challenge because they are not always allowed on local trains and buses. Good quality rentals are readily available at reasonable rates.

Cycling Around Japan: Road signs for cyclists can be found here. Read the cycling diary for updated posts on recommended itineraries; custom trip planning services are also offered. In English.
https://japan-cycling.com/road-signs/

Bikeshare Cogicogi: Rent from multiple locations of bikeshare ports and rental offices in Tokyo, Kyoto, Osaka, Fukuoka, Kamakura and Kamaishi starting at 2,400 yen a day. Cogicogi also offers electric models, long-term rentals and cycling tours. Download their app from the website in English and Japanese.
http://cogicogi.jp/smart/port-lang=en.html

Cycling Holiday Tokyo: Need a tour guide to ride with? Explore the back streets of Tokyo on a guided tour. Riders must be 12 years and older. In English.
https://www.cyclingholiday.tokyo/

Hubchari Osaka: More than 70 locations in Osaka make it convenient to rent a bike to get around in this metropolis. Register as a SMART member to use the bikeshare ports. If you are not a smartphone user, register as an ANALOG member and visit one of the two offices listed on the website to rent in person. Scroll down to the bottom for language settings in English, Chinese, Korean or Japanese.
https://hubchari-english.jimdo.com/

Cycle Kyoto and Osaka: See Kyoto by group tours, family tours, private tours or customized routes with an English speaking guide. Contact them by email to reserve a bicycle equipped with a child's seat. In English.
https://www.cyclekyoto.net/

Hida Satoyama Cycling: Experience *satoyama* up close by cycling through the countryside of the Hida area with a guide. The standard tour is 3.5 hours; custom tours available; also walking tours and winter tours. In English and Japanese.
https://satoyama-experience.com/cycling/

On the Road

Renting a car
Several reputable car rental agencies operating in Japan offer services in multiple languages, including online reservations to make prior to your departure. Most rental vehicles are equipped with a navigation system, but sometimes it can be an option. Be sure to reserve a vehicle with a system that can communicate in your preferred language; otherwise, the default language is Japanese. Navigation apps on smartphones work well in Japan. Another important option is the ETC card that automatically gets charged for tolls. For details, read the entry in this section about toll roads. Japan-Guide's website has a list of rental agencies (link provided under Helpful Information).

Renting a camper car (RV)
Growing in popularity is the chance to see the Japanese countryside in camper cars, or

RVs. Japanese camper cars can carry up to seven passengers depending on the make, but that number does not mean the vehicle can sleep that many, so confirm the sleeping capacity before committing to your selection. Navigation systems are usually included, and some are programmable in multiple languages. Again, navigation systems and other features can be extra options depending on the rental package you choose, so read the fine print. For a list of companies that rent camper cars, see Japan Recreational Vehicle Association's website (link to JRVA provided under Helpful Information).

Driving permit
Requirements depend on which country issued your driving license, so be sure to check the link to license requirements under Helpful Information.

It's different!
Drivers accustomed to traffic moving on the right side of the road will find driving in Japan a real challenge because everything moves on the left. Roads are narrower, congestion is everywhere in urban areas, speed limits are lower, parking is almost impossible and traffic signs are different. If you are bold enough to drive in Japan, do your research and learn all the important things you need to know about Japan's traffic safety and regulations well in advance of your departure.

Parking
Park only in designated areas. Do not park in empty fields, empty lots, or empty parking spaces that are not marked with a PARKING SIGN. You will be towed. And please, no sleeping in vehicles overnight.

Parking the camper car
Camper cars should look for parking spaces designated for trucks and oversized vehicles if the model you rent is a large unit, but wide parking spaces are not common. Parking in a public area for the purpose of spending the night in your camper is a no-no: parks, shopping centers, commercial retail facilities, ferry terminals and airports are off limits. So where can you spend the night? For the convenience of travelers on the road, more than 1,000 *michi-no-eki* (roadside stations) can be found throughout Japan. These roadside rest stops have large parking facilities, restaurants, markets, shops and special events. Not all *michi-no-eki* locations allow overnight parking and other comforts like bathing facilities, so be sure to check first before heading out. From their website (see Helpful Information),

search ahead to plan your road trip. There are a number of RV Parks in Japan, but the list from JRVA online is available only in Japanese as of this writing. The rental agency can help you find RV Parks near places you plan to visit. JRVA's website lists a number of dos and don'ts for parking safety and etiquette so do familiarize yourself with their advice.

Switches and stuff
Most Japanese car makes are equipped with turn signals on the left side of the steering wheel. Windshield wipers are usually on the right side of the steering wheel. Don't forget to turn off the headlamps when you park the car, just in case your model does not have an automatic shut-off feature. Be sure to acquaint yourself with the mechanics of the vehicle before taking off.

Hands-free is the law
To avoid fines and other serious consequences, do not use mobile phones without a hands-free device while driving. It goes without mentioning: no texting while driving. It is against the law.

Do not drink and drive
Driving under the influence of alcohol and drugs is a serious offense. DO NOT DRINK AND DRIVE cannot be emphasized enough.

Car seats for children
Ask the rental agency for a child seat if you carry a passenger under the age of six.

Roadside assistance
Rental cars are insured for repairs and damages so follow your agency's guidelines. Call the emergency number that was provided by your rental agency for instructions. Repairs done on your own might not be covered under the rental agreement so do not attempt to take matters into your own hands. If you stall, look for landmarks to describe your location. But first, pull off to the side of the road and turn on the hazard lights (emergency flashers). Place the reflecting triangle (there should be one in the trunk) behind the right tire so other drivers can see that you are stopped and need help. Or, you can raise the hood and hang a handkerchief from the window. Stay in the car and wait for a uniformed police officer or emergency personnel to come to your aid. If you have to leave the car: turn off the engine, unlock all the doors and leave the keys in the ignition. This allows emergency personnel access in your absence. Be sure to take your valuables with you! You must call the police if you are involved in an accident.

Toll roads
You can use the fast lane for ETC cardholders if your rental vehicle has an ETC card on its windshield (another thing to confirm at the time of rental). You can also rent the ETC card separately. Toll charges will be recorded on the ETC card and calculated for payment when you turn in your vehicle and card. Otherwise, make new friends with the person at the toll booth and pay as you go in cash (yen only).

No turn on red
There is no turning after stopping at a red light, so be sure to remain stopped until the light turns green again.

Driving in winter weather
Make sure your rental vehicle is equipped with winter tires if you plan to visit snowfall areas in the colder months. Major roads are plowed regularly but beware of unexpected road closures.

If you are pulled over
If a police car signals you to pull over, put on your turn signal and slowly come to a stop on the side of the road. Stay in your car. Do not exit the vehicle until so directed. Have your license and rental agreement ready.

HELPFUL INFORMATION

License Requirements: Driving permit requirements for non-Japanese citizens are published in multiple languages by the Tokyo Metropolitan Police Department. Click on MULTILINGUAL at the top of the page to select language preference.
https://www.nipponrentacar.co.jp/english/user-guide/driverslicense.html

Traffic Rules: Must-read information on rules of the road in Japan, traffic safety and tips for tourists provided by the Tokyo Metropolitan Police Department in multiple languages. Click on MULTILINGUAL at the top of the page to select language preference.
http://www.keishicho.metro.tokyo.jp/multilingual/english/

Japan Automobile Federation (JAF): Everything you need to know about driving in Japan as a resident or tourist. In English and Japanese.
http://www.jaf.or.jp/e/

Traffic Rules Explained: Skip to the JAF page on traffic rules and road signs. In English and Japanese.
http://www.jaf.or.jp/e/for-overseas-drivers/driving-in-japan.htm

Car Rental in Japan: Useful tips and what you should know in advance. Scroll down to LINKS AND RESOURCES for a list of car rental agencies operating in Japan. Set language preference from Japanese, English or Chinese at bottom of page.
https://www.japan-guide.com/e/e2024.html

Renting a Car in Japan: From "the site of choice for value hunters who want their yen to go further in Japan," a helpful article on everything you need to know before renting a car in Japan. In English.
https://tokyocheapo.com/travel/renting-a-car-in-japan/

All you need to know: Detailed information on renting vehicles in Japan from the website that is dedicated to "showing the charm of Japan to the world." In multiple languages. Scroll down to bottom of page for language settings.
https://matcha-jp.com/en/3609

Japan Recreational Vehicle Association (JRVA): Find your camper car rental here from JRVA's list of rental agencies. Be sure to read the Ten Commandments on how to behave in public parking areas. Select English or Japanese at top of page.
https://www.jrva.com/en/rental/

RV Life Magazine: Background information on RVing in Japan. In English.
http://rvlife.com/rving-in-japan/

***Michi-no-Eki* roadside rest stops:** Official website has a filtered search of roadside stations throughout Japan. Click on Michi-no-Eki Search. From the pop-up box, select your geographical area by prefecture and put in your filters. The search results will also give directions. In English and Japanese.
https://www.michi-no-eki.jp/stations/english

RV Parks: Locations and types of facilities available at 120 certified RV parks for the camper car traveller. Information in Japanese only.
https://www.kurumatabi.com/rvpark/list.html

Favorite Itineraries

This book is a collection of some of the best scenery from the far corners of Japan. Among them, the places on the following lists are special for reasons of their own. Trips to the shore, the mountains and *satoyama* can be most rewarding experiences.

Author's favorite views

Eastern Japan

Minuma (P15): Stroll through green space that provides environmental benefits for the Tokyo metro area.

Lake Hibara (P18): Your heart will flutter from close encounters with nature.

Izunuma (P19): Commune with the soundscape of the *magan*.

Biei (P24): Appreciate the artistic geometry on the hills traced by agricultural farming.

Akiyamago (P28): Nestled in an isolated valley, traditions and local culture have been preserved well. Heavy snow turns this area into a winter wonderland.

Azumino (P32): Take in the pastoral views of the highlands in the Japan Alps.

Western Japan

Fuden Pass (P42): Witness the fog descend and hear the winds howl for a most memorable experience. This natural phenomenon is a sign of the approaching winter.

Kumano Kodo (P44): The customs and lifestyle deep-rooted in a sacred environment evoke a serene atmosphere.

Lake Biwa (P47): Fascinating myths and legends add enchantment to the mystique of the largest body of freshwater in Japan.

Daisen (P52): Standing in the middle of the rice paddies, the little thatched-roof hut summons nostalgic sentiments for Old Japan.

Iya (P60): The sight of the village clinging to the side of the hill gives encouragement for humankind to persevere.

Aso (P70): The beauty of nature has many faces, as in the grandeur of the rolling plains.

Themed itineraries

Ski resorts

Lake Toya (P25): Hokkaido is a winter sport enthusiast's dream when it comes to powder quality snow. Windsor Snow Village, Niseko and Hirafu are close-by resorts. Snowfall levels are reliable in the winter.

Hakuba (P34): Great scenery, great snow, good access. There are a number of slopes that are suitable for all levels of skiers and snowboarders along the JR Oito Line. Tsugaike and Happo One get honorable mention.

Daisen (P52): Western Honshu gets less snow than the East, but Daisen has top ski resorts for the region. Views of the Sea of Japan are breathtaking from the mountaintops.

Fall colors

Okutama (P10): Outdoor adventures await in the hills just an hour's drive from the center of Tokyo. Immerse yourself in the colors of autumn, take the challenge to hike some of the advanced trails and pitch a tent overnight in the campgrounds.

Korankei (P40): More than 400 years of history makes this place near Nagoya a special stopover in the fall. Illumination at night starts in November and the Momiji Matsuri (Maple Festival) is also held during the month to celebrate the splendid beauty of *momiji*.

Takachiho (P74): Fall colors covering the deep gorges from top to bottom on a vertical plane around the main waterfall and trickling springs offer a once-in-a-lifetime view. Rent a small boat for the best views during your day trip from Miyazaki or Kagoshima.

Shrines, Temples and Pilgrimages

Tono (P20): The origin of many Japanese folk tales and legends, Tono is also the site of several shrines and temples. Visit Hagurosan, known for deep spiritualism, pilgrimages and *yamabushi shugyo* (rigorous ritualistic training). A temple stay (*shukubo*) can cost as little as 10,000 yen a night. Try the vegetarian cuisine of monks (*shojin ryori*).

Yoshino (P46): A World Heritage Site, the entire town feels like a religious compound. Detox for a few days here by visiting the area shrines and temples.

Views with an artsy flair

Owarabi Rice Terraces (P26): The rice stalks drying in the fields look like owls lined up in a row.

Uonuma (P29): Did someone stick the signposts in the snow?

Gokayama (P38): The lights in the windows of the thatched roof homes give off a warm glow, while the graduating blues in the background look hand-painted.

Fuden Pass (P42): The photograph captures a 3D effect of the fog wrapping around the whole mountain.

Aragijima (P44): The landscape is like a jigsaw puzzle; no missing pieces!

Oyama Senmaida Rice Terraces (P50): Reflections in the water-filled rice paddies are like polished panes of glass.

Hakata Island (P62): The shades of pink *sakura* in full bloom and the soft blues of the ocean and the sky combine to create a magnificent work of nature in pastels.

Hiraodai (P65): The "bubbling" earth looks otherworldly.

Aso (P70): Lush green plants grow in the mineral-rich volcanic soil.

Side trips and getaways

From Tokyo to Numazu (P14): A quick jaunt on the bullet train can take you on a luxurious getaway. See Mt. Fuji, dine on fresh seafood and *sushi*, visit an aquarium or soak in the hot springs. Take the Kodama bullet train (an hour one-way) or Tokaido Railway (less than 2 hours one-way).
More trips from Tokyo: Okutama, Yokohama, Kamakura, Miura, Hakone

Sapporo to Lake Toya (P25): Less than two hours on the super express from Sapporo is the seat of the 34th G8 Summit. Spend the night if you can to fully enjoy the farm-to-table experience with locally grown *wagyu* beef, exceptionally tasty seafood and fresh produce.
More trips from Sapporo: Biei, Furano, Otaru, Niseko, *Hakodate*

Nagoya to Lake Biwa (P47): A half-hour ride on the bullet train is Maibara. Take a taxi northbound on Sazanami Kaido (Route 185) to see Nagahama Port and the north end of Lake Biwa, known as Okubiwako. Eastward on Sazanami Kaido are pastoral views and Hikone Castle.
More trips from Nagoya: Hamamatsu, Ise, Toba, Shima, Gero Onsen, Gokayama, Takayama

Osaka to Kumano Kodo (P44): Kii Tanabe is just two hours from Osaka by train. If you can stay overnight, the Kumano Kodo pilgrimage experience will give you the honor of joining the travelers who have walked the same roads for over a thousand years.
More trips from Osaka: Kyoto, Nara, Kobe, Awaji Island, Shirahama

Kobe to Sanuki Fuji (P58): From Shin Kobe train station, take the super express bound for Shikoku for a 90-minute ride to Marugame station. See Sanuki Fuji, Marugame Castle and the stone walls in town, then grab a bowl of the famous *sanuki udon* noodles. Twenty minutes further on the JR line, *Konpira san* (formally Kotohira Shrine) near Kotohira train station is famous for the seemingly endless climb up the stone steps.
More trips from Kobe: Himeji, Shodo Island, Maizuru, Naruto, Iya,

Fukuoka to Aso (P70): Kurokawa Hot Springs and Tsuetate Hot Springs near Aso are within a two-hour ride on the highway bus from Fukuoka. Mt. Aso is one of the largest active volcanoes in the world.
More trips from Fukuoka: Dazaifu, Yame, Yanagawa, Karatsu

Anime and Manga

Near Okutama: The Studio Ghibli Museum in

the suburb of Mitaka is a must for *anime* fans. The museum is a virtual playground created by Hayao Miyazaki. See details on the official website. http://www.ghibli-museum.jp/en/

Near Miyama: The Kyoto International *Manga* Museum exhibits a historical collection of *manga* materials, including period pieces from the Edo era.
https://www.kyotomm.jp/en/

In Lake Toya: *Anime* cosplayers will enjoy visiting Lake Toya in June when the Toya Manga Anime Festival (TMAF) is held over one weekend. For 2019, the event is scheduled for June 22-23.
http://tmaf.toyako-prj.net In Japanese only as of this writing.

Sample itineraries

[**Explore eastern Hokkaido, an all season wonderland**]

Furano, Obihiro, Kushiro and Shiretoko are located in the vast frontier of eastern Hokkaido where nature abounds. Feast your eyes with panoramic views, long stretches of undisturbed landscapes and sightings of wild animals while sampling the local produce and fruits of the sea, and relax at a hot spring resort surrounded by natural scenery. Getting around Hokkaido is best done by car. Long distance bus service is an option, but the buses do not run on a frequent schedule so plan your transfers well ahead.

From Chitose Airport

↓ 3 hours

Furano Visit a lavendar farm. Taste some of the best milk and cheese products fresh from the dairy farms of the heartland of Hokkaido.

↓ 3 hours

Obihiro Go horseback riding at one of the many horse farms. Soak in the rare organic *moru* springs (thermal waters with plant material) at the famous Tokachigawa spa town.

↓ 2 hours

Kushiro Paddle a canoe through the wetlands. Ezo deer and the northern fox run wild.

↓ 2 hours

Akan *Marimo* (moss balls) grow naturally in beautiful Lake Akan. Great for angling and many other activities around the lake.

↓ 2 hours

Mashu Take a bus tour around the three lakes of Akan, Mashu and Kussharo to fully appreciate the beauty of undisturbed nature. Lake Mashu is one of the clearest lakes in the world.

↓ 1 hour

Shiretoko-Shari Enjoy nature-based tourism through eco tours of Shiretoko's five area lakes; choose from a range of well organized activities; or wrap up your trip with a leisurely lake cruise.

↓ 2 hours

Memanbetsu Airport Fly to your next destination.

[**Kansai Area, the heart of Japan**]

Five World Heritage Sites and seven of Japan's best landscapes are found in the Kansai region where history, culture, tradition and natural beauty offer a multitude of attractions. Communities bordering the choppy waves of the Sea of Japan have had to adapt their lifestyle to a harsh environment. By comparison, the tranquil and temperate waters have made a different impact on life around the Seto Inland Sea. Good connections between JR and privately owned railways make transfers very convenient on trains.

From Kansai International Airport

↓ 1 hour

Osaka Tour the city. Osaka is known as a foodie town. Try as many local dishes as you can.

↓ 30 minutes

Kyoto Immerse yourself in the splendor of this ancient capital and learn first-hand how shrines and temples shaped the history and culture of Japan. The gardens are beautiful in any season.

↓ 2 hours

Maizuru Lots to do in this area known as Kyoto by the Sea rich in naval history. Cruise the harbor, hit the seafood market, walk around the Red Brick Park, then go see Kongoin Temple and Tanabe Castle.

↓ 1 hour on Kyoto Tango Railways

Amanohashidate Considered to be one of *Nihon Sankei*—the three most scenic spots in Japan—since the Edo period, the sandbar stretching for almost four kilometers is said to be a divine bridge stretching to the heavens. Read more before you go at http://nihonsankei.jp/eng/

↓ 🚋 **90 minutes on Kyoto Tango Railways**

Toyooka Visit the sanctuary for storks that has successfully reintroduced the once extinct bird into the wild. Soak those aching muscles in the hot springs at Kinosaki, then stroll through town in your *yukata* (cotton kimono robes) provided by the hotel. But be sure to leave the *yukata* when you check out! Buy a bag made in Toyooka as a souvenir.

↓ 🚋 **1.5 hours by express on JR lines**

Himeji The castle should be the first place to go upon arrival. The many shrines, temples, museums and exhibits will keep you busy for a while.

↓ ⛴ **2 hours by ferry**

Shodoshima Olives in Japan! Comfortable year round, this island steeped in ancient myths is like an oasis with attractive features of both land and sea. Take the ropeway across Kankakei gorge. Maples are gorgeous in the fall.

↓ ⛴ **1 hour by ferry**

Takamatsu The portal to Shikoku welcomes you. Swing by Naruto and Iya before circuiting back to the airport.

↓ 🚌 **3.5 hours by Airport Limousine**

Kansai International Airport Fly to your next destination.

[**Kyushu: the *onsen* island**]

Some of Asia's most active volcanoes can be found on Kyushu. The constant flow of geothermally heated springs, steam rising from the ground surface and pools of hot water are typical to the landscape. Naturally, there are a great number of *onsen* spa towns, and here we introduce you to the best.

From Fukuoka International Airport

↓ 🚋 **30 minutes**

Futsukaichi Hot Springs The oldest spa town in Kyushu dates back to the 1300s. Be sure to visit nearby Dazaifu Tenmangu Shrine.

↓ 🚌 **1 hours**

Ureshino Hot Springs Famous for *yudofu* (hot tofu) cooked in spring water and Ureshino tea harvested in Saga Prefecture. Arita and Imari porcelain wares are named after the nearby towns from which they originate; a china lover's mecca.

↓ 🚕 **1.5 hours**

Unzen Hot Springs Boiling springs and steam spitting out of the earth give this spa in Nagasaki the name of *Unzen Jigoku* (Unzen Hell). Unzen was the first to market a heavenly spa experience to foreign tourists. Ironically, the boiling springs were used for torture in the 1600s.

↓ ⛴ **1 hour by ferry from Shimabara Port**

Kumamoto Stroll through Suizenji Garden built in the 17th Century and admire the impressive fortifications of Kumamoto Castle.

↓ 🚌 **3 hours**

Aso Take a day or two and try out the area's signature hot springs for comparison: Uchinomaki Hot Springs, Kurokawa Hot Springs and Tsuetate Hot Springs.

↓ 🚌 **3 hours**

Beppu This town has so many *onsen* spas that there are now eight districts known as *Beppu Hachiyu* (eight springs). Pick up a free brochure from the tourist information center at Beppu train station to see how you want to get to know all there is to know about hot springs: steam baths, steamed dishes, and even a *Jigoku* tour of geothermal features characterized into different types of hell.

↓ 🚌 **4 hours**

Miyazaki In Japanese mythology, the islands of Japan originated in Miyazaki. Nichinan Kaigan Quasi-National Park is a beautiful area along the coast, and the botanical garden in Aoshima has interesting specimens to study after a visit to Aoshima Shrine.

↓ 🚋 **4 hours**

Ibusuki Hot Springs Remember getting buried under a sand blanket on the beach? At Ibusuki, the blanket is a hot sand bath.

↓ 🚌 **2 hours**

Kagoshima Airport Fly to your next destination.

Now go have fun!

THINGS TO DO

Page	In and around:	*Sakura*	Hiking	Trails	Overlooks	Mountain Climbing	Swimming
8	Boso Peninsula	○	○	○			
10	Okutama	○	○	○	○	○	
12	Kaisei	○	○			○	
14	Numazu	○	○		○		○
15	Minuma	○	○		○		
16	Akagi	○	○	○	○	○	
18	Hibara	○	○	○	○	○	
19	Izunuma		○				
20	Tono	○	○			○	
22	Kushiro	○	○	○	○		
23	Toya	○	○	○	○	○	○
24	Hagurosan	○	○	○	○	○	
26	Akiyamago	○	○	○	○	○	
30	Nagaoka	○	○	○		○	○
32	Azumino	○	○	○	○	○	
34	Hakuba	○	○	○	○	○	
35	Southern Alps	○	○	○	○	○	
37	Noto	○	○	○	○	○	○
38	Gokayama	○	○	○	○		
39	Ikeda	○	○			○	
40	Korankei	○	○	○	○	○	
42	Fuden Pass	○			○	○	
44	Kumano Kodo	○	○	○	○	○	
46	Mt. Yoshino	○	○	○	○	○	
48	Miyama	○	○	○	○	○	
47	Lake Biwa	○	○	○	○	○	○
49	Nose	○	○	○	○	○	
51	Mushiage Bay						○
52	Daisen	○	○	○	○	○	
54	Ini	○	○	○	○		
58	Sanuki Fuji	○	○	○	○	○	
59	Nakatosa	○	○	○			○
60	Iya	○	○	○	○	○	
62	Hakata Island	○	○	○	○	○	○
64	Yame	○	○	○	○	○	
65	Hiraodai	○	○	○	○	○	
66	Saga	○	○				
68	Kujuku Island	○	○	○	○	○	○
70	Aso	○	○	○	○	○	
72	Nagasakibana	○	○	○	○		○
74	Takachiho	○	○	○	○	○	
75	Sakurajima	○	○	○	○	○	○

Fishing	Camping	Fall Colors	Hot Springs	Snow Ski	More things to do
			O	O		scenic railway
O	O	O	O		forest bathing, canoeing, rafting
	O	O			old farmhouses
O		O	O		water sports, shoreline cruises
			O	O		fruit picking
O	O	O	O	O	Keikoku Railways, cycling
O	O	O	O	O	lake cruises
	O	O	O		lotus blooms, birdwatching
	O		O	O	old farmhouses, folklore
O	O	O	O	O	canoeing, steam locomotives
O	O	O	O	O	canoeing, nature walks
	O	O	O	O	shrines, nature walks
O	O	O	O	O	highlands
	O	O	O	O	forest bathing
	O	O	O		fruit picking, wineries
	O	O	O	O	cycling, guided tours
O	O	O	O	O	highlands, wineries
O	O	O	O	O	salt farming
O	O	O	O	O	world heritage site
O	O	O	O	O	farm stays
O	O	O			shrines, temples
			O		pilgrimage routes
	O	O	O		shrines, temples, waterfalls
	O	O	O		world heritage site, shrines, temples
O	O	O	O	O	farm stays
O	O	O	O		cycling, lake cruises
O	O	O	O		cycling, farm stays
	O				fresh oysters
	O	O	O	O	horse back riding, livestock farms
	O	O	O		cycling
	O	O			castles, *sanuki* noodles
O	O	O	O		deep sea fishing
O	O	O	O	O	rafting, cruises
	O	O	O		cycling
	O	O	O		old towns
	O	O			hands-on crafting
	O		O		hot air ballooning
O	O	O	O		kayaking, shoreline cruises
	O	O	O		paragliding, volcano tours
	O	O	O		water sports
O	O	O	O		*kagura* theatrical dance
O	O	O	O		kayaking, old towns

ABOUT THE AUTHOR

Landscape photographer Takashi Sato majored in photography at the Tokyo Visual Arts College. Upon graduating in 1984, he studied under Takehide Kazami, whose artistic interpretations of mountain photography are renown. In 1990, Mr. Sato launched his independent career, capturing some of the most stunning images of Japanese landscapes since. In recent years, Mr. Sato has focused on subjects and vistas that are classically Japanese. His work has been published in several collections, and his exhibits include "In the Heart of Japan" at the Montreal Botanical Garden (2015) and other venues held in Japan.

Managing Editor	Yucaco Kimura
Copy Editor	Stella Colucci
Designers	Mieko Sato, Aya Funada
Illustrator	Aya Sakamoto
Special thanks to	Junko Yoshimoto
	Yosuke Takahashi
	Haruhiko Okura
	Hiroshi Kita
	Rumi Naito
	JETRO and Consortium Friends
	JAPAN campingcar rental center
	SMART GATE Inc.
	Digital On-Demand Publishing Center inc.

And last but not least, our sincere thanks to the members of the local tourist bureaus, visitor centers and various tourist organizations for their assistance and cooperation.

CONNECTING YOU TO WONDERLANDS
japan

2019年3月18日　第1版第1刷発行

著 者	佐藤 尚
発行人	木村由加子
発行所	まむかいブックスギャラリー
	〒103-0004　東京都中央区東日本橋2-28-4-2F
	TEL.050-3555-7335　www.mamukai.com

印刷・製本	中央精版印刷株式会社

Photography and text copyright ©2019 by Takashi Sato
Translation copyright ©2019 by Stella Colucci
All rights reserved.

Printed in Japan
ISBN 978-4-904402-18-4 C0026

＊落丁、乱丁本はお取り替え致します。
＊本書の一部あるいは全部を無断で複写複製することは法律で認められた場合を除き、著作権侵害となります。